DIARY OF A FLYING MAN

RANDY COHEN

DIARY
OF
A FLYING
MAN

ALFRED A. KNOPF
NEW YORK · 1989

THIS IS A BORZOI BOOK
PUBLISHED BY ALFRED A. KNOPF, INC.

Copyright © 1983, 1984, 1985, 1989 by Randy Cohen

All rights reserved under International and Pan-American Copyright
Conventions. Published in the United States by Alfred A. Knopf, Inc.,
New York, and simultaneously in Canada by Random House
of Canada Limited, Toronto. Distributed by Random House, Inc.,
New York.

Some stories in this book were originally published in somewhat different
form in the following:

The New Yorker: "When He Reemerges," "Diary of a Flying Man," "Dry,"
and "The New First Lady"
Gentlemen's Quarterly: "In Line," My Airspace," and "Backyards"
(originally "The Two-Lane Blacktop Road to Wry")
Harper's: "The Motel" and "Commuter Report"
Working Papers: "The Mom Squad"
Mole: "Man-Sharing"

Library of Congress Cataloging-in-Publication Data
Cohen, Randy.
Diary of a flying man / Randy Cohen.—1st ed.
p. cm.
ISBN 0-394-56124-4
I. Title.
PS3553.04257D5 1990
813'.54—dc20   89-45285   CIP

Manufactured in the United States of America
First Edition

FOR

KATHA

AND

SOPHIE

CONTENTS

···

········

v i i

DIARY OF A FLYING MAN

ARBOREAL
LIFE

One evening when you and your wife are feeling edgy, but not edgy enough for a quarrel, she'll ask: "Do you ever miss your life in the trees?" These are the lies you'll reply with:

Never. Other guys may yearn for their arboreal days, but not me. That life was damp, cold, and lonely. Barbaric. Moving indoors with you was the best thing I've ever done.

Sometimes, sure. But it's not really about the trees; it's about youth. Not regret, just nostalgia. Hey—I'd never give up my indoor life with you and the kids.

Not anymore. Oh, I liked it at the time, and when I was four I liked playing in the sandbox. But these days the life for me is indoors with you and our lovely furniture.

BREAKING WITH HOME: ERIC

Eric reacted differently. "I figured the hell with it, grabbed a few pairs of sneakers, and split. My wife was furious," he recalls, "but she survived. She's had the sofa reupholstered, and she

. . . .

3

sees lots of foreign movies. The kids complained at first, but kids are flexible. I know they're going to be crazy about it as soon as they develop some new friendships and a more powerful grip with their feet."

PICKING YOUR SPOT: GORDON

Your tree could be in the Amazon jungle, the vast expanse of Canadian woodland, Grant Park in Chicago, your cousin's back-yard in Louisville. Gordon's is on Manhattan's posh East Side. "Trees are the biggest plants in the world," he says, "and New York is also very big. Sure, some people call this life superficial, but what are they up to this evening? Reading Thomas Aquinas? I doubt it." Gordon's got a maple in the Sixties, right off the park, and he throws his clothes just anyplace. "They always seem to land on a convenient branch. It may look chaotic, but I know where everything is and how many times I've worn it." He's pleased that the streets are safe and quiet, the restaurants are frequented by fashion models, and the neighborhood is well maintained—no oak wilt, no white-pine blister rust, no bark beetles. "And no Mr. Fix-it for yours truly!"

A CASUAL ATMOSPHERE: JEFF

Downtown, Jeff lives in a ginkgo, a hardy ancient tree with the prehistoric style this bachelor prefers. "It's the last surviving species of a once flourishing order," he says with pride. "Mine's the one with the pile of beer cans at the base." In the trees, when you throw something, you've thrown it away. Jeff appreciates that informality: no pretensions, no curtains, no brooms. Unlike Gordon, he enjoys doing a little work around the place.

. . . .

"I've waterproofed my pornographic magazines with epoxy resins—*Playboy, Penthouse, Split Ends, Moist*—and to protect them from falling, I've anchored each one to a sturdy branch with galvanized chain."

SEX IN THE TREES: LEON

Leon enjoys abbreviated affairs with inappropriate partners. "I get intimate glimpses of lives I'd never see any other way, close-up looks at people who don't like me very much. It's fascinating!" At first, he was insulted that women wouldn't spend the night at his place, an ailanthus in Chelsea. "They complained that I didn't have wooden hangers, clean towels, a roof." Now he's delighted. "This way, in the morning if I belch, I belch." Leon relishes the spontaneity of arboreal sex: "out of the bedroom, out of my rut, and never during a key playoff game. But I wouldn't call it casual sex; there's nothing casual about it. I'd say that life in the canopy has made me tougher, and that toughness, paradoxically, has produced a new tenderness. I'm more willing to savor the afterglow, murmur endearments, and stroke her hair, looking for fleas."

THE NEIGHBORS: BRYAN

"It's a bohemian, anything-goes life," Bryan explains. "You meet all kinds of guys, a few birds, some insects, those little lizards." He has an oak in Central Park, so he sees a lot of mammals. "Squirrels, house cats, tree shrews, monkeys—not here, but in warm climates. And if you do move to a monkey area," he cautions, "you're going to have leopards. It's a trade-off." Most of Bryan's neighbors are nocturnal, so he can play the stereo as late and as loud as he likes. Some hibernate in nests in hollow trees, "but that's not my problem, unless I've lent them books or records." Some of them know nurses and airline stewardesses. None of them ever washes out anything by hand.

HAUNTED BY THE PAST: KEVIN

He remembers looking down at the top of his wife's head as she stood at the base of his tree, talking reconciliation. She spoke about couple-counseling, devotion, building a life together. "I thought about it for a moment, then I chattered and spat and pelted her with twigs."

DINING AMIDST THE LEAVES: GREG

Ten or twenty feet above your head, men are making dinner— a steak slipped into the broiler, something frozen popped in the microwave, things in cartons: Szechuan, ribs, a quick cheeseburger ordered up from the coffee shop on the corner. As they learn their way around the trees, men add fruit, buds and leaves, bird eggs, and small reptiles. "You don't need a hyperequipped kitchen," Greg asserts, "no nine-burner professional range. And no table." He eats in front of the TV, watching the game or something R-rated on Home Box. He shuns Tupperware, Ball jars, Ziploc bags. "I store the leftovers in my cheek pouches."

GETTING AROUND: JIMMY

He's acquired the powerful upper body of the orangutan; that means no sweltering in the subway, no flailing futilely for cabs.

. . . .

Jimmy swings through the trees at twenty, thirty, even forty miles an hour for short bursts. "It impresses the ladies," he declares. "But what really turns them on is the thick mat of hair that covers my back and chest. Sure transplants hurt, but I've mastered pain."

HEALTH: ALEX

Scampering from branch to branch is a perfect workout, building wind, balance, confidence. Alex has the firmest handshake of his life, thick seductive calluses, tough nails on all extremities; he wants more. "I'm a superachiever, handsome, successful, with many expensive cars and watches. I expect the best—a model type in her early to late teens, photo a must." His physician is administering certain synthetic hormones that will eventually give Alex a prehensile tail. "I worked damn hard for a lot of years, sacrificing for my family. I want something for me."

DEALING WITH CRITICISM: SLOW LORIS

"That's right: I'm sluggish, more sluggish than the true lemurs. You think I don't know that? Yeah, yeah, yeah—I have no tail. I sleep all day. At night I kind of prowl around looking for food—a young leaf, a tender shoot, maybe a bird egg. I don't have framed prints on the wall. I don't give little dinner parties. I haven't ironed anything since 1973. What kind of life is that? It's my life."

WHEN
HE REEMERGES

A QUIZ

You've got a terrible cold. Riding home on the bus, you feel a sneeze coming on. As you reach for a Kleenex, you notice that sitting across from you is Richard M. Nixon, the only American president ever to resign from office. Do you still cover your mouth?

At a dinner party you're startled to find him on your right. He says, "Pass the Triscuits, please." What do you do? Remember: the entree will be veal with a wonderful Sauternes sauce. Seated to your left is supermodel Elle Macpherson; Mel Gibson is across from you. They both find you wildly appealing. Stay or go?

He appears on "Sesame Street" to teach kids conflict resolution. He suggests: if you disagree with a playmate, get tough; threaten to set him on fire. Would you continue to watch "Live from Lincoln Center" on that same station?

You fall wildly in love and foresee a future of unalloyed bliss.

. . . .

Walter Cronkite, the most trusted man in America, comes out of retirement to do a single broadcast, exposing your fiancé as Richard Nixon. Having undergone reconstructive surgery at a secret government installation, he's thoroughly transformed, inside and out. These procedures cost billions of tax dollars that otherwise would have gone to rebuild our nation's crumbling infrastructure. Do you call the caterers and cancel the wedding?

A contestant on TV's "$25,000 Pyramid," you find yourself paired with the saurian former president. Do you give him good clues? Perhaps you deliver a stirring denunciation to host Dick Clark and stalk off the set? Suppose all the prize money goes to the Heart Fund? What if the Republican Party's elder statesman took you aside during the first commercial and personally apologized for the Christmas bombing of Hanoi? You're convinced he's really sorry. Dick Clark presents the first category, "Things dropped out of a B-52." What do you say to President Nixon?

SOME DOS AND DON'TS

Don't script a Nixon vehicle, even if you get a nibble at Disney from Michael Eisner himself. Can you spot the three dismal high-concept projects in the rest of this paragraph? Remake those classic Jerry Lewis movies with R.N. in the lead; start with *The Nutty Professor Is Not a Crook*. Update *The Man Who Would Be Imperial President* with Nixon/Kissinger for Connery/Caine; *Miracle on 34th Street 1969* with Bloomingdale's as Macy's and R.N. as a wiretapping Santa.

Don't lend him a three-cent stamp to augment his twenty-two if he's mailing a letter written under the pen name Senator Muskie's Wife.

. . . .

9

Don't hire the jowly unindicted co-conspirator to manage your American League East baseball team if he persists in seeing the other teams in the division merely as Soviet proxies. Do overrule him if you're leading Baltimore 3–2 in the ninth and he threatens to use nuclear weapons to block the route to the Orioles' bullpen.

HEY, KIDS, TRY THESE AT HOME

Pretend you're the ghost of Roy Cohn. (Ask your mom for an old bed sheet. Talk in a scary voice.) Invite Mr. Nixon for dinner at 21 and dancing at Regine's. Reminisce about the good old days with Joe McCarthy. Sneer at the stupidity of your critics— what a bunch of jerks!

In a singsong voice, chant something presidential as you jump rope. Think of rhymes for Operation Phoenix. Go Double Dutch: try rhyming executive privilege, protective reaction, Greek colonels.

Build a Play-Doh model of Cambodia. Drop cans of peas (ugh!) and beets (yuck!) and Spaghettios (yum!) all over it. Drop a canned ham on Phnom Penh. Then pretend your dog is on a Senate oversight committee; deny everything.

Use your crayons to draw a jail with Jimmy Hoffa inside. Now draw one without Jimmy Hoffa inside.

With flour and water and strips of ripped-up newspaper, build a model of President Nixon and of his national security adviser, Henry Kissinger. Have your new dolls make sophisticated chit-chat about silly things Daniel Ellsberg said on the telephone when he didn't think they were listening. Pretend your Nixon and Kissinger dolls are kneeling in prayer. What do you suppose they're praying for?

. . . .

ASK NIPPER AND CHIPPER,
THE CARTOON MORALIST BEAVERS

Nipper (voice of Cyndi Lauper) says, "Don't be a prig. You don't have to share a guy's politics to share a beer." (Nipper is the worldly one.) "Everybody makes mistakes. I'll bet there's plenty of stuff in your past you're not so proud of. Wait, there's the doorbell. It's Dick! Come into my lodge, pal. And look who he's brought—Attila! He scourged the known world. But hey, let bygones be bygones. Let's not dwell on the past. And look who else is here—enteric parasites. They've laid waste millions. What could they do? Bacteria got to swim, viruses got to fly. Besides, being nice to R.N. creates a lot of jobs."

Chipper (voice of Danny DeVito) says, "Oh, right—if it happened five minutes ago, it doesn't count." (Chipper is up to here with indignation.) "Hound that evil monster to the grave! And then throw stones at his statue!"

SOME HANDY PHRASES TO CLIP AND CARRY

For our noble cause, I would accept hors d'oeuvres from the Devil himself.

I'm just here to research this novel I'm writing. A few years from now. I keep a diary. When I remember to write in it.

It's easy to sit on your backside and criticize, but it's darn hard to topple Chile's elected government and dispose of Salvador Allende.

What do you call that jelly stuff? You use it to burn people to bits? It's like Saran Wrap?

It's those dirty rotten Jews from New York who are behind it.

. . . .

11

WHEN HE REEMERGES

Turn off the lights. Be very quiet. Hope he thinks there's nobody home.

Stand at closed window and mime: we've all got the measles. (Hint: sounds like "easels"; move your arms like an artist painting at his easel. It also sounds like "weasels"; kill a chicken and drink its blood.)

Say "We're just on our way out. Care to join us? We're going to blow up the neighbors' garage. We don't like their cat."

"I'm sorry; you can't come in. You were bad."

. . . .

THE HOTEL

The Ultrasuede sofa modules are gone from the lobby—smuggled across the border or sold on the black market. In their place are the backseat from a 1964 Plymouth, half a dozen orange vinyl beanbag chairs, and a few pieces of aluminum lawn furniture. A giant sea tortoise is used as a footstool. It keeps crawling out of the hotel and must be returned to the lobby several times a day. The swimming pool has been drained and filled with sacks of dried taro. "One never knows when such stores of the starchy root will be an enviable provision," comments the bellboy. As if to underscore his remark, there is a rattle of small-arms fire from the vicinity of the snake-rendering plant built a few kilometers from the hotel at great expense by Soviet technicians. Now, of course, there are no snakes to render.

The air conditioning is not working—some problem with the permits, some bribe that has not been paid. All sense of the exotic has fled, replaced by boredom and severe itching in the armpits and on the upper thighs. The elevator is out, too. Several of the capital's "moon flowers"—the local slang for copra

....

13

traders—use it as a place of business. Such things can be done here by slipping the night clerk a little "tandjung"—a caress of the private parts.

The bar still operates, although during this period of religious zeal it is considered bad form to order anything stronger than distilled water. In the middle of the room is an ash pile—the charred remains of coasters and cocktail napkins set ablaze during the worst of the fundamentalist rioting. The staff is too intimidated by the religious police, who are apt to drop in anytime with their holy books and truncheons, to clean it up. Despite the current tensions, Mr. Mobinda, the bartender (he is protected by a cousin in the Bureau of Fisheries), can be relied upon to provide swizzle sticks to favored customers.

There is talk of spies, but what is there here to interest a spy? Mr. Mobinda occasionally fences tiny radio transmitters in the shape of cocktail olives, but these are regarded more as a local handicraft than as espionage. There are rumors of the impending arrival of invading American marines, of Cuban volunteers, of mercenaries from Pakistan. Yesterday someone placed a set of those toy antennae with the glittering Styrofoam balls on the head of the tortoise. Is it just a harmless prank, or does it carry some sinister message?

Atop the hotel, above the fourth floor, is a rotating restaurant; it has never actually rotated. The motors are still crated on the docks. The treasury has no hard currency to pay for them, and their Japanese manufacturer will not accept dried larvae. There is talk of using water buffalo to rotate the restaurant, but as yet it is only talk. "What does it matter?" sighs Mr. Labuhan, the headwaiter. "We have no glassware, no table linen, no grapefruit spoons." Mr. Labuhan favors the Self-Sufficiency Plan proposed by the Ministry of Agriculture, which would convert the

· · · · · · · ·

At the airport, a recorded voice says, "The red zone is for loading and unloading only." But of course there is no red zone or any other color zone. There is just the heat and the dust and the vines that must be cut back each morning to prevent them from blocking the doors to the terminal. As the daily passenger flight lifts off, the tortoise plods across the runway; he has come quite far from the hotel today. The home version of an arcade video game is strapped to his back. Perhaps he'll make it all the way to the sea.

. . . .

IN LINE

Curtis loves that sense of community. "Remember in 1968,
you'd run into a lot of the same people at all the big demos?
Now I've got line buddies. Like Gene there—we met on line
for Bruce Springsteen at the Byrne over in Jersey, a ten-day
job. I met Cassie in Detroit, first time we were on network TV.
A big one, fifteen job openings at the Dodge Micro-Van plant,
the first thirty-day line in the Midwest. See the guy breathing
through the AirBoy? We spent weeks playing pocket-video gin
on a great discount mortgage line at a bank near Yonkers—23
percent if it was your first home. It was a real family line, plenty
of kids and hibachis. I've got playoff tickets–line guys and guys
I'm still pals with from the first water-ration line ever held in
Manhattan."

Louise also craves the good vibrations of the sixties. "Those
were the days of free rock concerts in the park. But things turned
stingy in the seventies, materialistic, and the key public event
became the flea market. By the early eighties, all the good stuff
had been sold, which was just as well because nobody had any

. . . .

18

money; stagflation hit hard. Everyone pined for things to bring us together—cataclysms. That's what we miss about the sixties—riots in the streets, mass hallucinations. Why do you think there's so much talk about nuclear war? To do away with it? We love catastrophe! Give me a hurricane, a flood, a power failure, and I'll give you America at its best as neighbor pitches in to help neighbor with only scattered looting in the outlying districts. The lines offer a taste of disaster with no contusions or abrasions. You preserve your dignity; you're spared the humiliation of scraping mud off your rugs on the network news while Dan Rather looks like he might go all teary. What's the worst that can happen in line? Maybe Crowd Control gets over-anxious and pops you with a tranquilizer dart; no permanent damage."

Carlo? He's crazy about the lines! "Especially now, with all the improvements. Things got a lot nicer since the Postal Service introduced its On-Line-Delivery special. Sure, at $29.95 it's a little steep, but compared with Federal Express, it's a bargain. Besides, you can put a lot of mail into that two-kilo pack. And how do you put a price tag on keeping up with your loved ones? You used to get a horrible sense of isolation after only a few weeks on an ultraline. Even when the first cordless solar phones came out, what did they give you—fifty or seventy-five meters? And you needed a scrip from your company therapist even to get on the waiting list. Back then everybody fought for a spot near the pay phones, remember? Now, with the extended-range models, you can 'Stay in Line and Stay in Touch,' just like it says in the commercials."

A couple of blocks down, the line bulges around a trash basket containing a cozy fire made from old newspapers rolled tightly by a Log-o-Matic.

. . . .

"It's the best thing to have with you," says Belinda. "It brings people together. Someone will have a few soy dogs, and there's always a spare turnip or two, and I've never been in an ultra when there weren't a few people with potatoes in their pockets. Soon there's eating and singalong and those good feelings you get at a real old-fashioned potato party. To me, that's what makes this country so special, the Log-o-Matic. It's the free enterprise system responding to the needs of the people in the day-to-dayness of their actual lives. It's why we have the Porta-Couch, the SaniMaster, Mr. Walls, Share-a-Shower, La Parsniperie."

Theresa loathes the lines, and she detests Curtis and Louise and Carlo "and that little bitch Belinda and her damn campfires. She's a line buff, man. People like that, they spoil it for the rest of us. There's a lot of people on this line not because it's some kind of potato party but because they've got to be here. I've seen Belinda in plenty of other lines. I remember the first time —I'm thinking, that cow doesn't need monoclonal antibodies; she's a stinking buff. She's going to make this line a week, ten days longer than it ought to be."

Harry defends the buffs. "They're artists with resourcefulness and ingenuity. They're why the lines are creative, exciting events. It's like back when they started the space program, and everyone said 'No, no, no! Too much poverty on earth!' But then we got Tang, the first orbital breakfast beverage, and people could see the good in it. That's what the lines are like. A lot of unexpected things have come out, things that are useful in everyday life, like the garbage-bag raincoat, the newspaper hat, the milk-carton waste-disposal unit. And what about the Log-o-Matic? Maybe it wasn't actually invented in a line, but it was field-tested and perfected out there."

. . . .

Mary Beth has washed out a few things at a fire hydrant, and she's hanging them to dry on the police barriers that restrict the line to the sidewalk and a single lane of the street. "I'm about as pregnant as it gets," she smiles. "*Muy* pregnant, as my friend Rita says. She says if your baby is born in line, it automatically moves up to first place. But I wouldn't plan a pregnancy around a line. Heck, if I'd planned this, do you think I'd have Douggie as the father? I just hope my baby will have advantages I never had, like a good, basic, trilingual education and adequate protective clothing."

Slats thinks the line builds character. "Some jerks say, 'Why don't they give everybody a number and let us go home?' What wimps! They don't deserve to be on this line. When my dad escaped from Bretska, he was willing to stand on a few lines to do it, and in steerage, too. Do you think he griped, 'Why didn't they give me a number back in Bretskapol?' Ha! At least in America a line leads to something, not just to cheap commemorative tureens imported from Albania. People today are such babies. They want everything handed to them. I say if a thing's worth having, it's worth waiting for, like sex or eggs or socks."

But Slats, what about those who hire the jobless to hold them a spot? Is this character-building exercise only for the poor?

"Don't ask me to knock this country," says Slats. "It's the best damn country in the world, except maybe for infant mortality and housing and literacy, but even there it's in the top thirty-five percent. If it's so lousy here, how come everyone isn't trying to break into Switzerland?"

You're at the end of a long, long line, Anthony. Is it worth it?

"Eye of the tiger, man! You got to have a dream, and you got to go for it. One time I took all my money out of the account, sold my car, sold my girlfriend's car, borrowed from all the guys, got a bank loan against my protein allotment, and laid it all on tickets for the $85 billion lottery. So maybe I didn't win, but I'm not discouraged. Fame! I'm gonna live forever. Besides, at any moment, this line could go alphabetical, right?"

MY AIRSPACE

The means I have available to defend myself are limited; mostly I rely on peer pressure. I look to the gentle authority of social convention, consideration for others, simple good manners, to deter commercial and military pilots from entering that imaginary cylinder that surrounds my body and extends infinitely upward—my airspace.

Lacking a sophisticated air-defense system—I am particularly weak in the command and control functions commonly provided by AWACS-type aircraft; I have no look-down / shoot-down radar—I must endure the frustrations of routine incursions by even the smaller airlines. Earlier this year, a Sabena flight bound for Brussels crossed into my airspace. If it was really bound for Brussels it was pretty far off course, overflying a route I employ to reach the Key Food market. Pilot error? Navigator miscalculation? Computer malfunction? Possible. So is espionage. Even if I possessed the means, I couldn't very well bring down a plane loaded with civilians, even a charter group, even Walloons. The publicity would be terrible. How would it sound opening the

. . . .

23

network news? "Late this afternoon, Randy Cohen of New York's Greenwich Village district downed a Sabena passenger flight, killing the two hundred forty innocent victims on board, plus three additional passengers whose innocence is still unverified. He's very sorry. He was under a lot of stress (quarrel with his boss). There may have been technical malfunctions." Right now all I actually deploy is rock-throwing capability, and I can't hurl one high enough or hard enough to significantly damage that type of aircraft (the popular A300 Airbus). So I endure these overflights, a humiliating slap at my personal sovereignty.

As difficult as it is to protect my airspace by day, the nights are worse; when I lie down, my airspace grows bigger. At least that's the theory I'm hoping will prevail in Geneva. Others assert that when one is reclining personal airspace vanishes altogether, being determined by the top of one's head. A complex formula is employed in which one plumb bob is hung from your nose, another is dangled from each of your ears. The triangle defined on the ground by these points is circumscribed; the resulting circle is projected upward as a cylinder, and there's your airspace. Preserve it, protect it, and always stand tall. If you slouch, it diminishes; if you lie down, it disappears. So they say. I say that my airspace is a bundle of infinitely high vertical lines rising from every part of my body. That's why I sleep on my side, to present the smallest possible target. I shun the provocative gesture; if I could sleep standing up, I would. Call me a horse; I only want peace.

Some people insist that for the sake of accuracy all measurements be made on the naked citizen. Others, more demure, insist on full drapery. But doesn't this invite cheating—suits with padded shoulders, conical brassieres, broad-brimmed hats?

. . . .

Won't some favor giant clown shoes, pneumatic slacks? There are many such disputes to be settled. What happens in a fifty-story office building? With so many executives crisscrossing above and below one another, how to determine who controls the airspace? Won't the uncertainty provoke unendurable anxiety in those subject to the territorial imperative, testosterone poisoning, or overidentification with their corporate status?

All agree that where no one stands—parts of the Bronx, vast stretches of the Gobi, the icy expanse of Baffin Bay—is international airspace. But even here there is discord. Some say that a person's airspace stops at his nose; others claim dominion two hundred miles beyond their epidermal limits. The latter view prevails in coastal areas, at the edge of the rich fishing banks and mineral reserves of the outer continental shelf. If you were about to grow wealthy on kelp or cod or manganese nodules, you too would seek to restrict overflights well beyond your layer of subcutaneous fat.

Each stakes out his borders and provides what protection he can. A popular passive measure is wrapping a mat of pink fiberglass insulation around your head; it displays only a muddled profile on enemy radar. Active measures include battle-tested Stinger missiles strapped to your back. You may find this approach unnecessarily bellicose, and it is certainly uncomfortable when you sit, particularly in Broadway theaters. The people behind you will have a hard time seeing the stage. Those folks paid forty-five dollars a seat, and they might have full retaliatory capabilities, so why look for trouble?

I try to stymie overflights with the application of an obsolete air-defense method, counting on the element of surprise. I've rigged a harness, anchoring above me at various heights barrage balloons of the sort that helped win the Battle of Britain. Any

. . . .

craft violating my airspace ought either to ram a balloon or entangle itself in the lines. But so far my system has always failed. All incursions happen thousands of feet above my top balloon. And the harness is an awful nuisance whenever I take the bus.

Over on Horatio Street they've formed a block association to defend their mutual airspace, chipping in to hire a World War II surplus P-51 Mustang. It flies intercept missions above the neighborhood—from the playground, out past the Greenwich Twin Theater, over to P.S. 41, then back to the playground. Right now they can afford to send out sorties only about once every six weeks, but next month they plan to have a bake sale. Thanks to the bingo, they've begun shopping around for a battery of SAM-6 missiles, the nice, heat-seeking kind. They'll deploy them on the roof of the apartment house at 32 Horatio if the super gives his OK. Once they've trained on the SAMs, I expect they'll sell those old ack-ack guns mounted on top of the greengrocer's. I'm hoping to pick them up cheap, maybe go in with a couple of the guys. We could take turns.

The president of that pricy new co-op down on Eleventh Street has been hinting that his building will deploy ground-based particle-beam weapons, a spinoff from the SDI program. They're expensive and probably won't work, but he insists that by maintaining an R&D program—they run it in the building's health club—they'll have the bargaining chip they need to negotiate a route change for Continental's Baltimore-to-Buffalo flight. He's been a lot less belligerent since the October '87 stock market plunge when he came inches away from losing his job. Since then, he's had to moderate his life-style—less expensive wines, off-the-rack suits, and no stealth technology for the car. He drives a sporty little Datsun two-seater; I think it's leased.

In an ideal world, I'd follow the example of Saudi Arabia and

. . . .

purchase the advanced mobile air defense system known in Arabic as the Shahine, or Falcon's Eye, featuring six French Crotale antiaircraft missiles mounted on an AMX-30 tank chassis. But talk about expensive! And that alternate-side-of-the-street parking could drive you crazy, not to mention trying to find a space during the day in midtown. Yes, I know I could park it in a garage. Sure—for $285 a month. If I want to come back and find half my guidance system missing and my paint scratched.

But it's not an ideal world, is it? It's a world where SR-71 Blackbird surveillance aircraft traveling at Mach 3.32 cross into my airspace at 85,000 feet. It's a world where every pipsqueak TV station operates its own helicopter (to keep an eye on the commuter situation, they say). But despite these repeated provocations and routine violations of my territorial integrity, I remain steadfast: I will never—never!—be the first to employ nuclear weapons. I'm just not that kind of guy.

DIARY OF
A FLYING MAN

Mankind's oldest dream has become my reality: I can fly. This morning, running after a five-dollar bill blowing along the pavement, I simply lifted into the air. What profound transformation will my life undergo? Unfortunately, the five turned out to be a torn page from Sunday's fashion supplement, "Traditional Tweeds: The Courtroom Choice for Ex–City Officials." And just before I soared skyward, I stumbled and got an oil stain on my trousers. At least I hope it's only oil and not PCBs.

Testing the limits of my astonishing new power, I flew to the dry cleaners to pick up my pants. They still have a faint stain on the knee, like a ghostly silhouette of Donald Manes.

My first flight to work reveals the city as more than a chaotic pile of limestone and steel. I watch enraptured as streets and skyscrapers organize themselves into what is undeniably some patternlike shape!

City scandals undermine morale in many agencies, even here

. . . .

at the Pools and Playgrounds Planning Board. To lift our spirits, the boss, Mr. Kauffmann, posted a sign: MORE THAN ____ DAYS WITHOUT A WORK-STOPPING FELONY ARREST. As he updated the count to eleven, I smiled, delighted that in a mere three hours I'd be flying to lunch.

I can cruise comfortably only at a walking pace. With effort I can attain running speed, but just for short bursts. From now on, only light beer. If I could sustain higher velocities, that would change everything. Of course rain would still be a problem, particularly when I'm carrying groceries: those plastic bags really dig into your hands! What was wrong with plain old paper bags? Why can't things stay as they are? Ah—my unprecedented aerial gift has made me introspective.

Mr. Anselmo, my landlord, is complaining about my coming and going from the roof. The thumping disturbs the top-floor tenants, and I'm causing leaks in the tar paper. Now I'll have to walk to that parking lot near the piers. It's inconvenient, but what can I do? To take off from the ground, I need to run about a block and a half. Well, if I leave fifteen minutes early, I can still fly to work.

Windy day. Got a bit airsick during the commute, so I did the last half by subway.

Home. In the mail was a summons to jury duty. Threw it away. After all, I am a flying man.

Mr. Kauffmann caught me doing personal work at the office. One of my bench designs. This one has armrests shaped like a sphinx with the head of Bess Myerson, and legs with the trim

. . . .

ankles of the former Miss America. Its feet are shod in high-heel pumps. It's the best yet in my "Under a Cloud" series. Someday, each corner of Broadway, from Inwood to Battery Park, will have a bench honoring a former Koch official. That'll show Kauffmann. Besides, once the indictments are handed down in the BenchTech investigation the city will start handling bench designs in-house, maybe from our office.

Flew to Yonah Schimmel's for those delicious cherry-cheese knishes. They were all out, so I had apple.

Cruising uptown, I was surprised to see so many rooftops littered with old refrigerators crammed with review copies of bestsellers, eventually to be sold at the Strand, I suppose. Even in our throwaway age, recycling thrives.

A few blocks later, I glanced down and saw a crew of uniformed firefighters hand-fitting mosaic tiles on the rooftop love grotto of an assistant deputy mayor. On city time! A big one glanced up and hollered, "What are you looking at, creep?" I hope he didn't recognize me. Maybe I can use my fantastic skill to nail some of these guys.

Out flying around. Forgot to turn on phone machine. I wonder if anybody good called.

Flew to cash machine on way to work. It was out of order, so I flew to another. It took three more stops before I finally got my money. I couldn't even use a customer service phone to complain: some busted, some stolen. I shall write an angry letter. My fabulous ornithoid prowess makes me less passive in the face of institutional authority.

Then, far below me, near the Williamsburg Bridge, I spotted

. . . .

some cops napping on the job. With their little sleep masks in place, three or four assistant police commissioners dozed in hammocks slung between their squad cars. Sleazy! Circled until I felt dizzy, which made it really hard to take notes.

I dropped my notebook on a guy! It just grazed his shoulder, but he was furious. I gave a phony name, Chadwick Lancaster, but you could tell he didn't believe me. I wish I could think faster. As I flew away, he gave me the finger. I snapped back, "Oh yeah? Same to you, stupid!" Has my unbelievable supernormal talent taught me nothing?

"Accidentally" dropped a half-gallon of skim milk on the roof of a taxi. Then I bombed a limo with a thirty-two-ounce jar of applesauce. I am not bound by the laws that govern ordinary mortals.

As I glided home after work, some guy clambered onto the roof of a Jews for Jesus van and harangued me with a bullhorn. He asked if I was Jewish, and the easiest way to avoid an idiotic conversation was to say no, but then I felt guilty.

A creature of the skies, I've learned to observe the urban ecology. At the edge of a vacant lot a pack of feral hamsters reduces a cat to its skeleton in seconds. Or else it was a bunch of kids in Davy Crockett hats stripping a car. Above eighty-five feet my sense of scale is unreliable.

Hovered over Central Park watching a riding mower cut a vast Mercedes-Benz insignia into the Sheep Meadow, like a huge chlorophyll billboard. Adjusting my Nikon, I nearly crashed into a tree. I've got to get one of those autofocus cameras.

. . . .

My excursions among the spires lift my spirits, reminding me that nature endures, even in the metropolis. On fire escapes and in window boxes the first vegetables of summer are ripening. Say what you will about bioengineering, those beach ball tomatoes look delicious, although if one fell it could crush a Subaru.

Five crime sightings today. One payoff, three kickbacks, a bribe. The new telephoto lens is bulky, but it takes a great picture.

If I had a way to carry luggage, I could fly to Fire Island for the weekend. An in-flight snack would be good, too. Smoked almonds. And some kind of beverage.

When the infrared photos came back from the lab, I saw that Thursday's sighting was not a bagman, just the kid from the deli delivering a roast beef sandwich. I'll amend the logbook.

Got really tired flying to work today, so I snatched a ride on the roof of a bus. Cost to me? Zero.

Early evening, soared over Queens. There was a deb party in Shea Stadium. A bar was set up in each dugout; buffet tables lined the base paths; heedless teen socialites capered on the pitcher's mound. But I thought the stadium was closed all week for resodding? Then I saw a borough president trundling a wheelbarrow full of cash across right field out beyond the 410 feet sign and into his official car. I'm going to rip this town wide open! And I got all the evidence I need before the wide-angle lens fell into the bullpen.

At the office I tripped over a trash can, churning up records of Kauffmann's involvement with a cabal of civil court judges.

. . . .

They're conspirators in a crooked franchising scheme to install cigarette machines atop jungle gyms in city playgrounds and underwater in city pools. That's it. I'm going to the papers.

My meeting with the reporter wasn't all I'd hoped for. She does want the story, but she can't get to it for a while. Next week she's assigned to the wicker supplement. And after that, she'll be filling in at "Buying and Owning."

A social disaster! Had a big date with Leslie, a new designer at the office. I whispered, "Let me fly you to the stars on wings of love," and then I jerked her off her feet and dropped her on the coffee table. That's it. I'm cutting out pie altogether, and tomorrow I start working out with weights.

No Nautilus machine can help me now: my powers are fading. How can I resume ordinary life having known the embrace of the air? I am desolate.

Awoke with odd flickering at the edge of my field of vision. Gradually I realized what was happening: I'm developing X-ray eyes. Already I can nearly see through a sheet of newspaper. This will irrevocably rend the drab fabric of my life.

Kauffmann resigned! He wants to spend more time with his family for reasons of health while going into private consulting at a major university to do the teaching he loves. Perhaps I misjudged him.

False alarm. Just a malfunctioning fluorescent lamp. Otherwise, my vision is what it's always been: OK in right eye, slightly astigmatic in left.

. . . .

33

No mistake this time: I can move objects with the force of my will—telekinetic power. So far I can't budge anything heavier than a few pounds, and my range is restricted to about four feet, but still! After breakfast I slid the *Sgt. Pepper* CD (Can it really be fifty years? Oh. Twenty years) across the coffee table. I brace for the unimaginable metamorphosis my life is about to undergo. May I use my new power wisely!

. . . .

COMRADE
ENTERTAINMENT

Remember *Clucks Deluxe? Legs Ahoy? The Cockeyed Caballeros?* Well, hold on to your hat. It's Muggs and Skeezix, those lovable lollapaloozas, making more movie mayhem in *Lobster Pots.* As Der Mugger himself would say, Yipsky-Pipsky!

You laughed your pants off at *Ach, du Lieber St. Augustine,* the slap-happy sendup of Martin Luther that introduced their pal Dimly Johnson, the nutty Norwegian who'd do anything for some smoked herring. Flemish painting of the sixteenth century? Only *Boy Oh Breughel,* Muggs and Skeezix at their antic best—trouble at their heels, a song on their lips, and a gaggle of gorgeous gals just around the corner. And there was never a gal more gorgeous than Linda Purcell! Is she in *Lobster Pots?* You bet!

So come on along with Linda, Dimly, Muggs, and Skeezix to naughty, nautical New England, a rugged land where sinewy farmers wrest gnarled potatoes from the rocky ground, throwing back those deemed too small so they can mature and spawn, breeding the next generation of russets. But what

. . . .

about the lobsters? Did you say lobsters? There's seafood aplenty, neighbor, so grab your sou'wester: time's a-wasting!

There's something bittersweet about this 1949 trailer: *Lobster Pots* was the last Muggs and Skeezix movie. Although the gang never again worked together, separately they flourished. Linda stayed in the business, did well, married better, and now lives in Palm Springs where she is very close to Sinatra. A fixture on the evangelical prayer-breakfast circuit, Miss Purcell remains a staunch friend of Israel. Dimly opened a Norwegian restaurant that became the cornerstone of the world's seventh-largest franchised food operation. Skeezix concentrated on his singing but still found time to make a fortune in real estate, building extruded-concrete tube-houses out in the Valley.

As for Muggs, he went solo with *Pie and Ivy, Stairway to Rhythm, Dateline Dixie*. But pictures had ceased to be his first love. What he really enjoyed was putting together a flashy show—the girls, a singer, a first-class band, maybe a novelty act, and then a few more girls—and taking it on the road to entertain the workers and peasants. It began with the spectacular he produced for Mao Tse-tung's army retreating toward Yenan. It was 1935; Muggs had just finished shooting *Rangoon Romeos*, but the guy wouldn't rest. And Mao was glad he didn't.

"We couldn't have made the Long March without him," Mao confided to a reporter from *Life*. "An army travels on its funny bone," he quipped, "and on memories of Paulette Goddard."

Muggs remained characteristically modest. "Hey, it's those kids in the people's armies who deserve the credit," he insisted. "I've been in this business long enough to know that you can't smash imperialism to the tune of Paul Robeson singing 'Ol' Man River'! You want morale? Give them laughter and legs—and I don't mean Lillian Hellman's."

. . . .

Muggs mounted his biggest show just outside Hanoi before the Tet offensive in '68. Jerry Colonna was the second banana, and oh those beautiful dolls—Ann-Margret, Raquel Welch, and the young and lovely Brooke Shields, only three and a half but already a dazzler.

Most people don't know that Muggs and Ho Chi Minh go way back. It was in Paris; you wouldn't believe how long ago. Muggs was an unknown hoofer, and Ho had a job painting "Chinese antiquities." They met for the first time at the stage door of the Crazy Horse Saloon. Each of them had flowers and candy, the whole bit. Yep—they were waiting for the same girl. Then a limousine pulls up, the girl trots out of the theater, and she drives off with another guy. Instead of putting up their dukes, the boys went out and got drunk and ended up pals for life. So when it came time for Tet '68, Muggs flew out the entire chorus line, the Girls of the Crazy Horse, for the show. Ho was touched. "Muggs is a beautiful, beautiful guy," he said. "He's brought a lot of pleasure to a lot of people."

The Cuban shows have always been special, ever since Muggs did the Sierra Maestra in 1957. Jane Russell was on the bill along with Fess Parker. Fidel called Muggs "one of the nicest guys in the business."

Sam Goldwyn called Muggs "a traitor, a disgrace to the industry." Muggs loved to get Sam's goat. That same year, as a prank, Muggs hung a replica of Sputnik from the chandelier in Goldwyn's office. Later, after Batista fled the country, Muggs whispered it around that he was buying the New York Yankees and moving the team to Havana as a gift to the revolution. Goldwyn nearly choked on his Dominican cigar. "When it comes to loyal Americans," he said, "include Muggs out."

Politics aside, there was a warmth to Muggs that drew people to him. You know how JFK could be about Castro, but that

. . . .

37

didn't stop him from inviting Muggs to the White House, seating him between Pablo Casals and Robert Frost. It was Jackie's finest hour as a hostess, smoothing over some rough social sledding. People ask if Muggs fixed Jack up with girls from the show. Who can be sure? The President himself said, "It's a privilege to have worked with Muggs, and I mean that from the heart."

Before the Democrats recaptured the White House, Muggs palled around with Ike, and, if you believe the D.C. gossip, it was Der Mugger who first cautioned Eisenhower about the military-industrial complex. "But he never took my advice about using a nine-iron when you're twelve yards out from a well-bunkered green," said Muggs, "or about seizing the means of production and returning them to the proletariat."

"Everyone knows he's a friend of anticolonial insurrection," said Ike, returning the compliment. "But few people realize how hard this crazy guy works raising money for the Kidney Foundation."

Which isn't to say that Muggs didn't have his problems. Nixon harassed him, LBJ made crude jokes about him, and Wayne Newton refused to work with him. Throughout the fifties the TV networks kept their distance, so he had to use crews from the BBC or Télé-France. He hated Soviet production teams. Their cameramen shot Jayne Mansfield as if she were a dancing bear, he declared, and their directors had rotten timing, cutting from his face to take a reaction shot just as he delivered a punch line. The first show he did with a Russian crew—Pyongyang, 1950 —was a disaster. "Comrades," Muggs moaned after yet another joke fell flat, "I may be the only comedian invited to be buried in the wall of the Kremlin, but I hadn't planned on dying to-night."

Not all of his critics were on the right. Gus Hall accused Muggs

. . . .

of charging exploitative rates to act as spokesman for the United Electrical Workers. And he took a lot of flack for his famous—and as he would later admit, sexist—TV commercial for the ILGWU when he had a ridiculously hard time finding the union label inside the clothing of a leggy Vegas showgirl.

Naturally Muggs could dish it out, too. In 1954, asked his opinion of Pete Seeger, he snickered, "Pinky-pinky, plinky-plinky," miming the motions of banjo playing. "Just because I support the progress of world socialism doesn't mean I want to sit through thirty-seven verses of 'Michael, Row the Boat Ashore.' Lenin would have tossed this guy off the sealed train." More recently, Muggs developed a similar aversion to Jane Fonda, despite his assertion that she was brilliant in *Any Wednesday*.

What next for Der Mugger? He'll be taking a troupe to El Salvador for a cable special. There's talk of reuniting Muggs and Skeezix, Linda and Dimly for a golf tournament to raise money for the American Cancer Society and *The Nation* magazine. And, if glasnost goes just right, he'll be on the reviewing stand in Red Square, two guys down from Gorbachev, for the Macy's May Day Parade. Retire? Not likely! Ol' Muggsinsky is one of the hardest-working people in the business with a schedule that would exhaust a guy half his age. And that's just the way he likes it. No wonder they call him Comrade Entertainment.

BACKYARDS

I was exhausted. I needed to get away, to light out for the territory, to reconnect with the real America, the one along two-lane blacktop roads, preferably in disrepair. I craved the rough-hewn wisdom residing in towns with populations under 7,500 and willfully eccentric names: Gee Gaw Gumbo, Louisiana; Donkey Mustache, Utah; Inky Dinky Spider Down Your Pants, Kentucky.

Unfortunately, there wasn't a small town on the continent that didn't have a contract with a major publisher, no colorful coot without a commitment to Charles Kuralt. And so, packing a few necessities into my car, a '79 Buick Electra I'd named Alexis de Tocqueville, I began a voyage that would take me from suburb to suburb, by backyard across America.

MAPLEWOOD, NEW YORK

"Popsicle Pete doesn't come around anymore," Dee Dee Daniels tells me when she comes outside to say good night. I was surprised how readily the Danielses had assented to my request to pitch my tent out by their pool. Clearly, I'd underestimated the kindness and generosity of the American people. (Fully 82.6 percent of us in the USA are kind and generous, I read on the top of a pile of newspapers stacked by the Danielses' garage for collection by the scouts. Now I had names.)

"Not for years. He was run out of town in 1975 when he got caught dealing fireworks and pornography out of his truck."

These days, if you live in Maplewood and want a Fudgsicle, you drive over to the 7-Eleven. Life is change. But it is still a Fudgsicle when all is said and done. The Danielses understand this almost instinctively; they shed no tears for the Popsicle Petes of bygone days. And I, after years of Häagen-Dazs rum raisin, am beginning to see it, too.

CRESTVIEW, OHIO

Lulled by the sound of trucks passing on the Interstate, as rhythmic and soothing as waves crashing on the shore, I sit on the Kurtzes' redwood deck, sharing a Tab with my hosts. There is serenity here, an ease embodied in every detail of their lives. Consider the aluminum-with-nylon-webbing lawn chairs on which we sit. Like the furniture in the traditional Japanese home, they are brought out only when needed; when not in use they are stored away in the garage, near Jack's cache of automatic weapons. But America is a land of progress, and this virtue too is present in our lawn furniture. To clean, simply hose them down. What's more, this chair is so light that a child can carry it, although when unfolding it, often as not he'll pinch his fingers.

"A little Bactine and a Band-Aid soon put matters right,"

smiles Jack Kurtz, a man unruffled by life's little vicissitudes. How differently we'd respond in Manhattan. We'd sue.

PINE RIDGE GARDENS, INDIANA

Resting on the flagstone patio of the Tilghman family, I use my binoculars to watch the ten o'clock news through the window of their rec room. (My lip-reading skill, perfected while observing the marital squabbles of the couple across the air shaft from my apartment, is proving valuable.) I notice that my hosts eschew store-bought cigarettes in favor of rolling their own. There's the frugality, the self-reliance so esteemed by Emerson and Thoreau! And to economize still further, the Tilghmans take deep drags and hold the smoke a long, long time. Wise husbanding of resources! Those who associate such thriftiness with a dour temperament are surely in error, for the Tilghmans are a frolicsome pair, giggling constantly, even at the weather report. Blithe spirits! Americans!

PLEASANT GLEN, IDAHO

Up early for a brisk wash in the Lindners' birdbath. It was necessary to crack the ice that coated the surface; conditions are rougher than I'd anticipated. Still, I had the fortitude to decline their offer to sleep in Oscar Lindner's hobby room. (It is rare to see such an extensive collection of Third Reich memorabilia outside a museum.) Sticking with my plan to lead the outdoor life, I made camp over by the swings. I did accept Oscar's loan of his Norelco cordless razor. I can share his enthusiasm for its rotary heads. A close shave! And how liberating to be rid of the cord, to cut the umbilical that would bind me to the house. I

. . . .

had a sensation of true freedom I'd not known since the day
my final divorce decree came through. Here is unfettered man!

CASA BUENA ESTATES, CALIFORNIA

When Bud and Betty Enslen took me to Cap'n Eddie's
Surf'n'Turfeteria, I expected only a break in my Spartan routine
of cooking on borrowed briquettes. But as we walked up to the
salad bar, I saw not just the canned chickpeas, the pickled beets,
the bacon bits, the creamy Roquefort-style dressing; I saw the
limitless bounty of America. For the first time, I apprehended
the phrase "amber waves of grain," and I knew that our skies
were truly spacious, our plains indeed fruited. Simple fare? Perhaps. But it was a decent honest meal, redolent of the productive
might of our fields, farms, and factories. And Cap'n Eddie offers
identical dining in thirty-two states, a unifying force binding us
into one nation, one folk, one culture, just like the pledge the
Enslen kids say at school. From sea to shining sea. With a choice
of beer, wine, or sangria.

SUNNY MEADOWS, TEXAS

I lie in my sleeping bag in Stan and Janet Gilbert's backyard,
gazing at the stars and listening to the conversations from the
cocktail party flowing around me, and hoping nobody would
step on my stomach in the dark. Janet Gilbert says that a powerful backhand is essential to a good game of tennis and proudly
describes her own progress in mastering this skill. Off to my
left, someone suggests that it must be difficult to improve your
game by taking lessons in a motel room. Surely this is so, and
one must admire her all the more for persevering in such

. . . .

cramped conditions. The strength of will that enabled her fore-
bears to settle this vast Texas prairie is still very much alive,
over by the big satellite dish, sipping a blue margarita. (I later
learned that Janet's family never traveled west of Reading, Pennsylvania, but the theory still holds.)

As I listen to these people chatting and laughing, I feel a
renewed confidence in our nation and its citizens. They abide,
they endure. Each morning waffles are dropped into toasters,
and kids are dropped off at school. Soon they'll grow, apply for
their learner's permits and, if they pass the written test and can
parallel park and nothing turns up in the urinalyses, be off into
the world.

And tomorrow morning I too will be off to another suburb,
another backyard—off into the heart of America.

. . . .

SLEEP
PROBLEMS

Carl can't fall asleep: he fears small-scale spontaneous combustion—the grain in his bird-feeder will burst into flames, searing an unwary sparrow, setting the apartment on fire. During the day, he knows that such pyrotechnics are unlikely, so he doesn't remove the feeder. But at night, when he is about to drop off, he worries and awakens.
Advice: Avoid spicy food near bedtime.

Holly passes turbulent nights: she sleep-knits and fixes on her rivals—is she falling behind? "It's terrifying," she laments. "I wake up, and there are eleven feet of powder-blue modacrylic something. It's not a scarf; it's not a sweater: I don't know how it got there or what the hell it is. OK, I know how it got there —I've seen the film they shot at the Sleep Center, so I realize that I made this . . . thing. But I don't even know how to knit!" Holly fears that while she spends herself on this stuporous craft-work her rivals will sprint past her, working through the night. "They'll win the awards, the glory, the plum assignments," she

. . . .

wails. Holly admits that even her fiercest competitor must sleep. "But," she snaps, "I'm damned if I'll ask how many hours or what kind of blankets."
Advice: Open a window to ensure good ventilation.

Wayne makes lists. Soon after he turns off the light, another item occurs to him that must be written down. He has a special pen with a built-in light so he won't disturb his wife. It doesn't help. His lists vary; currently atop the pad on his night table is the heading "Datsun versus Dachshund." Below this: "both small; both produced by former Axis powers; four wheels / four paws; inanimate / animate; radio standard / radio unavailable, but you could probably attach one to the collar with string." It's a wonder his wife hasn't walked out long ago.
Advice: Stuff rags under the door to provide the silence essential to proper sleep.

Lois, asleep, wishes ardently to be French or at least Swiss. Awake, she's sickened by her nocturnal longings. Each session of her group therapy features small savories from a variety of countries. "Everyone is so polite and encouraging," Lois reports. "They go, 'This sharp cheese is excellent! What noble people to devise such a dairy product! How admirable is your policy of armed neutrality!' It helps a little."
Advice: Remove overly exciting books from the bedroom or cover them with brown paper bags.

André has other people's dreams, mostly those of S. Dillon Ripley, former secretary of the Smithsonian Institution: falling, flying, appearing naked before a PBS documentary crew, sorting memorabilia of imaginary presidents—Henry Bessemer,

. . . .

Thomas Carlyle, Isaac Hayes. André is bored silly by Ripley's nocturnal drift, except for a dream involving Michelle Pfeiffer and some odd nineteenth-century folk art, and he is annoyed to have the dreams of a man with a first initial rather than a real name.

Advice: Align your body along the polar axis, with your head to the north, or tape powerful magnets to the bedposts.

Connie's postal obsessions keep her up for hours. "I worry how long the lines will be at the post office tomorrow. Did I put enough postage on the letters I mailed today? Did I casually apply a stamp that will be worth thousands to collectors in thirty years? Is it unethical to use the Rutherford B. Hayes commemorative when I disapprove of so many policies of his administration, particularly his use of federal troops against striking railroad workers? It's all so trivial, but my mind grinds on. Then I panic: if I don't fall asleep right now, tomorrow I'll be too tired to get anything done. At that point I'm doomed. I get up, put on my robe, go into the living room, phone someone I loathe, and threaten them in a disguised voice, usually this high-pitched nasal twang."

Advice: Before retiring, pack the legs of the bed in ice.

Amelia and Don have trouble sleeping together. "It's my fault," says Don. "I sleep great with women I don't love, but I can't fall asleep with Amelia around." She tries to be understanding, but Amelia too is dissatisfied. "Don thinks that I drop right off, but I don't. I've never been able to. I only pretend to be asleep. And he's so easy to fool—most men are—that I grow contemptuous of him." They're being treated in the Sheep Meadow in New York's Central Park with a therapy they've written them-

selves. Amelia says, "We didn't want the experience to be just a lot of fancy words nobody understood."
Advice: Houseplants emit healthful oxygen when their pots are wrapped with high-voltage cables.

Lucy found a support group in the Sleepy Time Gals Clarinet Orchestra. "We all studied at the Sleep Center," she explains. "It was a sort of therapy. We hoped it would regulate our breathing or perhaps send soothing vibrations through the jaw to solve the clenching problem." Some had played clarinet in their high school marching band; others were beginners. As the orchestra improved, dissension developed: would they perform publicly, and if so, in concert or on parade? And if on parade, should they be high-stepping strutters or something more somnambulistic? Should they commission new compositions? Should they admit men?
Advice: Coat floor and baseboards with epoxy paint, and pump six inches of sea water into the bedroom.

The sleep-disturbed inhabit their own culture of self-help workshops and longed-for bedding breakthroughs. Their newsletters warn of quackeries—soporific sheets, Slumberine facial mist, Lethargel creams and ointments. Thousands have been gulled by the Lactolier, the light-bulb equivalent of seven glasses of warm milk. Each night, the nocturnally hampered sleep a lot more than they realize, and each day they fail to understand how they could have spent so much money: they just went to the bank, and already they're out of cash. The sleep-dysfunctional claim famous figures as members of their own afflicted tribe. President Garfield tossed and turned all night, they insist, probably from sleeping on the too-soft mattresses of the day.

· · · · · · · ·

Throughout the golden age of television, Peter Lind Hayes drowsed during "The Stork Club" whenever he wasn't actually on camera. Edvard Munch took uneasy naps in a tub filled with spoons. The sleep-challenged speculate about what early sufferers might have achieved had they been evenly matched with their better-rested contemporaries. It is widely held that the Collier brothers would have been impressively tidy, either on the federal bench or in figure-eight auto racing.

There is reason to hope. At the Yuri Gagarin Neurosomnology Laboratory near Novorossiysk on the Black Sea, Soviet scientists are amassing clinical data on electro-assisted sleep, infant aquasomatics, morpheotic nightwear. There is a facility outside Kansas City where technicians extract bodily fluids from hibernating bears, dormice, badgers, and bats. Construction has begun on what appears to be a vast indoor prairie dog village. Perhaps experimenters will synthesize key secretions of these winter sleepers. The FDA pledges vigilance. A Sunbelt senator promises expanded federal subsidies. A top East German somnologist has defected. During his last press conference, the surgeon general yawned sympathetically.

Advice: Adults should get eight hours of undisturbed sleep each night.

MACH
SPEED

For almost the entire month of April 1989, noted author, journalist, and TV personality William F. Buckley, Jr., will host
what will surely be, short of flying to the moon, or beyond,
the most exhilarating trip of anyone's lifetime. A supersonic
record-setting journey, aboard a privately chartered British
Airways Concorde, to destinations that surpass the mere exotic. We'll be staying at some of the best hotels in the world,
and be welcomed with the kind of receptions usually reserved
for royalty.

[Mr. Buckley] . . . will also be providing political and cultural commentary throughout the trip.

The cost is just $39,000 per person . . .

—advertisement, *The National Review*

New York. Giddy with anticipation, I board the rented Concorde
with the name Whittaker Chambers proudly emblazoned across
her nose. As I sit down, I notice that the great man himself has

. . . .

written the entire in-flight magazine and the instructions on the airsick bag. In twenty minutes, just that morning. In the car on the way to the airport. He keeps a printing press in the trunk, manned around the clock by a Salvadoran servant who's been with the family for years, taking his meals, sleeping, raising his children in various limousine luggage compartments.

Acapulco. Our polymath host demonstrates the strictly voluntary emergency procedures. Fasten seat belts if you wish; smoke all you want unless your seatmate is carrying a pistol, and if so, good luck to him. Gun control isn't the business of the FAA. Mr. B travels with big jars of flammable liquids—paint thinner, cleaning fluid, kerosene: it is his right as a free man.

Oakland. Exotic indeed.

Honolulu. We endure the loyalty checks good-naturedly, a small sacrifice of personal freedom to keep our little flying nation safe from those who might harm us, or who wouldn't fit in. (I tap the side of my nose.) Some of the older passengers request that the electric shocks used to refresh our memories be of a slightly lower wattage. Babies.

Kona. Every voyage has its characteristic sounds, its associated scents. Our odyssey harmonizes the muffled roar of jet turbines with the pungent aromas of ink and flesh. As we go supersonic our on-board tattoo artist busily prints the required warnings on passengers' bodies—homosexuality, Hebraic tendencies, belief that everyone in an advanced industrial nation should have basic medical care. Mr. B defends our right to these ideas, just so they are clearly declared in twelve-point type.

Papeete. Today he slouched way back in his chair and made that supercilious rabbit face. I'm in heaven! Short of voyaging to the moon or beyond—say to Venus or, yes, one of the outer planets, even Pluto itself—I can conceive of no greater ecstasy.

. . . .

I've talked to guys who stood atop Everest, who picked up Nobel prizes, who shared a good cry with Oliver North; when I told them of my impending journey, they didn't even *try* to hide their jealousy.

Christchurch. While this is the *most* exhilarating trip of my life, it's not the only time I've been exhilarated. I went to the mall to pick up a leaf blower with Norman Podhoretz ($950). I floated down the Mississippi in an armed bass boat with Pat Buchanan ($2,500 for an afternoon; $500 extra to use the deck gun on anti-apartheid shanties when we passed college towns). I drove to Disney World with George Will and family ($11,000), stopping at every damn Stuckey's on U.S. 1 so the young conservative could buy another pecan log. Just outside Baltimore he offered cultural commentary. "I loathe this song, but I can't get it out of my head: 'Don't worry; be happy!' Yeah, right."

Probably not Queenstown. Mr. B's been navigating by the seat of his pants (an expression he seems unwholesomely fond of); nobody's sure where we are. Today we received the kind of reception usually reserved for royalty, but fortunately, the national police had sufficient supplies of tear gas to curb the worst of the rioting. Say what you will about foreign aid; American police training is efficacious. Mr. B was inspiring, warding off rocks and bottles with his laptop computer. He has the catlike reflexes of a seasoned sailor and regular Ritalin user. "It's better than going to sleep every afternoon," he said, and using his keyboard as a shield, he escorted us to the palace of the President-for-life, pausing only to offer a police dog an affectionate pat on the head.

Sydney. The stitches came out today, leaving Mr. B's hand swaddled in a tidy bandage where the policeman's Alsatian bit him.

· · · · · · · ·

Perth. We've got a stowaway! Most of the passengers say he's a reactionary teen brat, but Mr. B finds him charming. The boy had gotten into mischief, roughing up a teacher whose pedagogical methods were insufficiently rigorous. Mr. B is letting him work his passage as a flight attendant. He looks darling in the little tunic, done in Dartmouth's colors. His picturesque ethnic slurs have a nostalgic feel, harking back to the days of the minstrel show. Mr. B loves music.

Colombo. Trouble with our lovable thug. He keeps referring to his fellow stewardesses as "a yammering pack of sluts." They're all threatening to quit. Youthful high spirits, says Mr. B reassuringly; he's just tugging the rabbi's beard, and maybe clubbing him to the ground, and sort of kicking him in the spine.

Mombasa. I love the clickety-clatter of the word processors that fold down from our seatbacks when we go for another record. Today's attempt—most ways to recycle a newspaper column. I came up with college lecture, hardcover anthology, speech to corporate big shots, banter with Larry King, slogan on comical coffee mug. The previous record, no surprise, is held by Mr. B himself. He once wrote a column that he quoted in full the next week; the passage of time had made it yet more relevant.

Masai Mara. Naturally, there is keen interest in the doings of our sesquipedalian cicerone. I won today's pool by guessing the number of times he'd use a multisyllabic Latinate word when a short Anglo-Saxon one was available.

Cape Town. Another stirring encounter with the great man. He was ambling up the aisle, collecting the headset rentals as is his nightly habit. *"Karate Kid II?* It's a Kung-Foolishly good time," he said, with a bow to what he's called the "lethal verbal powers" of Mr. Gene Shalit. Smart travelers rent the headsets even if they've seen the movie because the other audio channels are pure bliss. Channel 7 offers Mr. B reading from his own works. So do 3, 4, 6, and 17. He reads stories for kids on 14; I especially like "McCarthy and His Animal Enemies." And everyone loves the Abe Rosenthal comedy channel. "One of the funniest men living," Mr. B asserts. Like he has to tell us! If your appetite for mirth remains unsated, try Channel 13 for the comical dialect stories of Joe Sobran, "one of the two or three wittiest men I have ever met," says Mr. B. "Oy vay!" as Mr. Sobran would put it, albeit with better timing than mine.

Monrovia. Once again he refuses to turn on the air conditioning until we each reaffirm our faith in the divinity of Christ.

No way this is London. I didn't know air-to-ground missiles could be mounted on a Concorde, but that's just one of the educational tidbits you pick up traveling with history's greatest author, journalist, and TV personality—except when Thomas Jefferson appears on a David Frost special alone. What with the noise of the explosions, I missed Mr. B's political commentary when we stopped—well, not exactly stopped, but flew low and slow over Managua. OK, so technically it wasn't a Soviet tank battalion, it was a foundling hospital run by Maryknoll nuns, but the rockets worked great! That's the kind of technological know-how we need to recapture world markets.

New York. Exhilarating? Like flying a laser sled to the spiral nebula in Andromeda!

....

PANDA-MAN

Despite his sex problem, we all adore the panda-man; he is in short supply, he is very cute. We have no home-grown panda-men; they are flown in from an East-bloc country when a thaw in relations permits. This panda-man lives in Washington. He is particularly cherished on slow news days. He eats exotic leaves. He resembles a giant teddy bear, but he is not a member of the bear family. He's related to the ferrets and mud snakes. He is kin to the Norwegian brown rat. He has a pouch.

This panda-man will not reproduce. Perhaps he can't face adult responsibilities? Perhaps he is reluctant to abandon the sans-souci style of his bachelor days? Perhaps his own childhood was bleak? Perhaps his sperm lack speed and motility—a result of industrial by-products in the groundwater, a result of his witnessing a nuclear test, a result of the large amounts of lead in the air due to auto emissions? Perhaps he surreptitiously employs a contraceptive device? Perhaps he has had a vasectomy? Perhaps he has unusual powers of self-control?

This new panda-man in town is named Gkltphing-Gkltphing.

. . . .

He spends his days eating exotic leaves and his nights enjoying idiosyncratic sexual encounters with a series of panda-women flown into town by their backers in the hope that the pair will hit it off in a substantive way. So far, nothing.

His newest friend is Bdnjsving-Bdnjsving. She lives in the Dallas–Fort Worth area, although, like Gkltphing-Gkltphing, she was born in the East bloc. Their love affair is a product of the improving atmosphere between their nation and ours. From time to time, we receive a panda-person to help us with our slow news days and to promote cultural exchange and the trade in heavy industrial equipment and thickly enameled cookware. We also receive many crates of exotic leaves.

Gkltphing-Gkltphing and Bdnjsving-Bdnjsving sip melon liqueur and dance to Sinatra records. "In the wee small hours of the morning . . ." coos Ol' Blue Eyes to swaying panda-people. They are quickly adjusting to life in the capital. They have developed their own unauthorized channels of communication within the Department of Transportation; they have reliable, unofficial sources at the General Accounting Office. They permit lobbyists from the oil and natural gas industry to buy them lunch and automobiles. Bdnjsving-Bdnjsving shipped her automobile, a Camaro, back to the Dallas–Fort Worth area; she gets around Washington in Gkltphing-Gkltphing's Porsche 914, a gift from those pleased with his efforts to prevent additional taxes at the wellhead.

In other cities, other panda-people are aware of these events. Pptahcl-Pptahcl resides in the twin cities of Minneapolis–St. Paul and enjoys the winter weather, finding shopping convenient, no matter how chilly the day, in the many stores linked by the skywalk. Nfwij-Nfwij resides in the Tampa–St. Pete metroplex and is a little anxious about the alligators, although she's never

. . . .

actually seen one. Owing to this fear, she declines all invitations to play golf. She is a frequent guest on local talk shows and is now growing her own premium brand of exotic leaves. She will pack them in embossed gold foil boxes for the holiday season and market them to other panda-people across the nation. This will solve their gift-giving problems. She carries on a lively correspondence with formerly convicted felon Claus Von Bulow, begun during his first pretrial hearing, and she is delighted that the dapper millionaire was at last acquitted. Perhaps one day they will meet in Palm Beach for cocktails. He will sit opposite her; Henry Kissinger will sit on her left; Donald Trump on her right. Someone will stroke her instep with the toe of a gleaming English wingtip. Who?

Panda-man of the moment, Gkltphing-Gkltphing has recently dined at the White House, sharing a table with the leader of a small nation, the president of a large corporation, Loretta Lynn, the little brown ones, and Alf, the lovable wisecracking alien. Gkltphing-Gkltphing enjoys hearing Alf say "No problem!" on TV, and performs a wicked impression of that evocative catchphrase. He can also imitate Sanyo's newest line of talking appliances—"Your four-grain bread is golden brown, my good friend"—and Alan Alda, the beloved Hawkeye. This panda-man is a deft entertainer with a waggish streak and a flair for japery! That's what they said in *People* magazine when they declared him one of the year's twenty-five most intriguing concepts, along with number 11, Pentagon Procurement (photo: crew of a B-1 bomber submits to drug testing); number 6, the Savings and Loan Bailout (caricature: officers of Texas banks hold specimen bottles); and number 19, New Parks Policy (computer drawing: privately owned moose undergoes drug screening).

Last week fifteen dump trucks filled with sand were moved

. . . .

away from Gkltphing-Gkltphing's residence and replaced by a
barrier of refrigerator-freezers filled with top cuts of beef. Security depends upon surprise: panda-man eats no meat, and a
slab of frozen flank steak will stop most small-arms fire. Later
the freezers will be removed; a deep ditch will be dug in their
place and stocked with vipers; trained dogs will be deployed in
imaginative ways. Panda-man knows of no particular threat, but
rest assured routine steps will be taken to protect him from
deranged ideologues capable of hurling sacks of medical waste
into his yard to dramatize their fanatical stance.

Cultured, genteel panda-man, a fine friend of the arts, takes
a journey to Doggerel Ranch, a grant-supported versification
center in the high desert out beyond Newhall, California.
Gkltphing-Gkltphing is pleased to discover that the ranch, a
popular retreat for urban aesthetes, is located near Vasquez
Rocks, where the popular television program "Hopalong Cas-
sidy" used to be filmed. In panda-man's language, this cowpoke
is called "Skvrnjl." When Gkltphing-Gkltphing was young, he
enjoyed the Western adventures of Hoppy and his horse, Topper
("Vtlmp"), dubbed into the regional dialect. During the ceremony of welcome at Doggerel Ranch, young poets present
panda-man with gifts—images of light, snow, glass, angels, the
sky, anomie, water on rocks, geese flying south. He reciprocates
with cultural samplings of his land—artfully embroidered na-
pery, dogs' teeth intricately carved by dental students, delicately
textured handmade paper plates, a twelve-tone symphonic work
that invokes the spirit of large-scale smelting operations. Later
he will ride a palomino along a mesa, mosey over to the chuck
wagon where exotic leaves will be barbecued, offer insightful
critical comments at a poetry workshop.

This panda-man is an excellent goodwill ambassador; he is

. . . .

at home on the range. He is equally at ease escorting a chic panda-woman to a Verdi opera or a degrading live sex show, attending a disarmament conference or depantsing an upstart, sampling cuisine minceur or accompanying local police as they make many arrests at an illegal dog fight in a nondescript garage in a quiet neighborhood. Truly panda-man is a citizen of the world.

Back in the District, panda-man braces himself for soul-wrenching nostalgia as he opens a letter from his cousin Rmtjl-Rmtjl in the old country. Life goes on in Gkltphing-Gkltphing's absence: the leaf crop is bountiful, no babies are born. The USC Power Frisbee team, his opposite number in the cultural swap that brought him to America, has played an exhibition match in his hometown, sparking enthusiasm for this modern game of speed, agility, aerodynamics. However, a lamentable ignorance of advanced injection-molding techniques has restricted availability of the colorful plastic discs. Attempts to provide adequate substitutes from the plentiful supplies of cymbals, stockpiled for the nation's many military bands, have resulted in serious wrist and neck injuries, providing many occasions for survivors to display the dark humor so characteristic of the region.

The season's new television programs have reaped general acclaim. Cousin's favorite show is "My Little Margie" (in the dubbed version, "Dmntvsk Yklxa-Yklxa"). "That little scamp is always falling into the soup," observes the cousin, "with comical consequences."

Gkltphing-Gkltphing puts the letter down. Such parochial concerns! He is unstirred by these tales of home; he feels no pangs. He is an American now, occupied with larger matters. What is the proper balance of conventional and nuclear forces in this new era of U.S.-Soviet relations? What polymer-based

. . . .

film will best protect his Porsche from the corrosive effects of road salt? Stick with cassettes or switch to CDs? Such questions would be meaningless to his simple cousin. Gkltphing-Gkltphing feels himself drifting inexorably away from his own past. This is not an unpleasant sensation.

DRY

CHEYENNE, Wyo.—Four and a half tons of county and private records, waterlogged in a historic flood, have been dried out in a special vacuum tank.

—New York Times

Mr. D'Achinda knows the moment that transformed him from an exile into an American. "It was the first time I dreamed not in the language of my birth but in the parking lot of a shopping mall. Or perhaps it was the instant I realized I no longer had a favorite recipe for the succulent tuber of my boyhood village but loved over all others one service area on the New Jersey Turnpike, the Admiral William F. Halsey. The HoJo Cola there is most highly carbonated; a brief immersion will restore the luster to a Roosevelt dime."

A modest insight perhaps, but Mr. D'Achinda has become a humble man. A document reprocessor specializing in the safe, thorough drying of water-damaged papers, he travels the in-

. . . .

terstate system in a truck fitted with elaborate equipment, much of his own design. He restores deeds and death records saturated in flash floods; he rescues library books soaked by faulty sprinkler systems—"or those triggered by teenage boys in an excess of testosterone vigor," he says, chuckling indulgently. Once, when the pipes burst at a Kamera Kwik, he saved thousands of vacation snapshots. "I returned many to the wrong envelopes," he admits, "but I believe that no one noticed."

Just as the American representative promised a decade ago in the besieged provincial capital, Mr. D'Achinda and his countrymen now dominate this field, finding a niche between the Korean greengrocer and the Greek coffee shop. "Not that I trusted this fellow," says Mr. D'Achinda. "To deal with governments is to confront harsh self-interest. You must expect deceit, treachery, toxic fluids poured into the irrigation system at the experimental soya farm, a popular nightclub performer called upon to shatter the patella of an outspoken critic of the President-for-life, the duty-free importation of Steven Spielberg films crudely dubbed into the seventy-two distinct dialects of your small and troubled country, with accompanying plush toys."

But this time the promise was kept: the American resettlement effort was generous and efficient, benefiting many officials of the old regime. Mr. D'Achinda smiles appreciatively as he drives across I-80 near Wilkes-Barre, Pennsylvania, comfortable on his lumbar-supporting cushion. His little cardboard pine tree freshens the air; his Fuzz Buster radar detector eases the mind; his heating coil plugs into the dashboard whenever he wants a steaming mug of *tskutar*. "And," he adds, "I have a place high on the waiting list to install the vital organ of a monkey into my Uncle Bahor in exchange for one of his own.

"How my uncle smiled when we arrived at our new home,"

. . . .

Mr. D'Achinda continues, "its concrete anti-terrorist barrier tactfully disguised as a bird feeder. Astonished by the diversity of your newsstands, he was particularly impressed with *Celebrity Sleuth's* 'Network Nudes' magazine, rhapsodizing over the breasts of Donna Mills, Abby of TV's 'Knots Landing.' Soon he adopted several stray cats. He trained one of them, a big orange tom named Spiro, to soil the editorial page of the *New York Times*, disdainfully stepping over *Post* and *News*, *Newsday*, and that pink paper, to reach his intended target. Uncle Bahor won many barroom bets with this stunt, a protected form of political expression in his new land."

Mr. D'Achinda worked and saved, and soon he had the money for his own truck, purchased from a prosperous countryman who was graduating to a bigger vehicle. (He had grown rich drying out bales of C.E.O. love letters in the Romantographic Room at *Forbes* magazine.) They conducted their transaction in the old way. "But because I have no wife," Mr. D'Achinda explains, "my neighbor Louise Pahlavi prepared the special foods. Babette Thieu—she owns the Liquor Pit down the road—brought a bottle of *tsamar*. This truck was just a little Jeep Wagoneer. On the side I painted the star and crescent and the name Susan Sarandon. I was in business. I would have taken our guests for a drive, but Spiro had soiled the passenger seats."

Mr. D'Achinda took what work he could find, anyplace the little truck, Susan Sarandon, would carry him. "I must have dried a thousand acres of double-knit quilts, sodden in unexplained plumbing mishaps in isolated Midwestern farmhouses. Such pipe bursts were generally blamed on Jewish bankers, their methods unspecified. Once, when things were slow, I dried the hair of all the contestants in the Wee Little Miss Missouri Pageant. Another time, I was summoned to a Nevada hotel suite

. . . .

to dry a wallet dropped into the bathtub by Mr. Howard Hughes. He paid me seven thousand dollars, though he could have easily done the job himself with his toaster."

There was no vacuum tank then, no DocuDry letterhead with its smiling-piece-of-paper logo. There was only Mr. D'Achinda in his silver suit, clumsy surplus gear once used by aircraft carrier fire crews. His hands protected by asbestos mitts, he'd heft the heat gun and stride toward a mountain of wet paper. "I seldom slept the night before a big job," he recalls, "although I gobbled dozens of E-Z Doze. I was too nervous; there was so little margin for error." It seems humorous now, but it was hard to laugh when, knee deep in the ashes of N.E.H. grant applications, he faced an angry mob of psychohistorians outside the flooded mailroom of Ohio State University.

Mr. D'Achinda persevered. He experimented with microwaves—eleven of the biggest ovens he could find, ganged together in the bed of a pickup. The rig was a menace, scrambling TV signals, jamming pacemakers, stunning mosquitoes until they drifted hubcap high around the truck, a Chevy longbed he'd named Sword of the Prophet and decorated with a drawing of Jessica Lange. In North Carolina near Camp Lejeune, he brought down a Marine T-40 trainer. "My lawyer calls it pilot error." In Memphis, he confronted the terrible consequences of seepage in the vault beneath Graceland. "I was able to save many room-service receipts from the King's Vegas period."

Even with his improved drier, papers in the middle of the pile stayed damp. On the huge microwave railway cars G.E. executives tackle that problem with teams of avid young apprentices who cheerfully clamber in among the paper with their long rakes, eager to keep these entry-level jobs that ensure their stay in this country. How could D'Achinda vie with the radar train?

· · · · · · · · ·

Its sheer size was intimidating: it could dry a vice-presidential archive in an afternoon. "Still," he reminisces, "it was exciting to challenge the giant. You cultivated speed and agility and the resourcefulness to wedge a chunk of scrap metal into the switching equipment, stranding the train on the edge of St. Jo for days, while you swept into town and demoisturized thousands of King Hose beefcake calendars, fund-raisers for the volunteer fire department."

More vexing were the franchise outlets, the Dodge mini-vans with the grinning face of Mr. Dry Guy painted on the side. "I understand the yearnings of these retired couples with their small savings, their mysteriously insolvent pension funds, their licensed handguns and tight-lipped suspicions nursed for thirty-five working years. They want to be useful, to see America, to avoid the spare bedroom of their children. It is a heroic thing to cruise into a town with your nationally advertised service and evaporate the sewage runoff from the files of the police department's Contraceptive Squad. But how can I compete with these old fools? They must merely meet expenses until they drop dead one day—maybe a stroke on I-75, the Mr. Dry Guy van drifting slow and deadly over the medial strip into oncoming traffic. I must make a profit, feed a family, build a future. Can I be blamed if late at night I use a small fire extinguisher to smash portions of their motor?"

As Adam Smith predicted, competition sired innovation. Mr. D'Achinda converted from microwave gear to the modern vacuum tank. Hauled on a trailer behind a big White Freightliner, his tank maintains the low pressure necessary to dry papers at temperatures under 75 degrees when the seals hold. He's painted a scimitar on a front fender and named the truck Melanie Griffith. This is the rig he drives across I-80, heading for Iowa

. . . .

where heavy rains imperil first drafts throughout the Poetry Workshop Belt.

Regrets? "Uncertainties, perhaps. There was a moment—this was years ago—when I could have destroyed all copies, scripts *and* score, of Broadway's *Cats*. I had only to turn the heat gun a degree or two higher. Otherwise, my life is good." Mr. D'Achinda smiles. "If only N'Djina, my driver back home, could see me so happy behind the wheel. But I'm afraid he could not jump high enough to grab the strut of the departing helicopter."

. . . .

MY MODELING

I was tall and slim with a wild mass of blond curly hair. Surrounded by the mob of cavorting dogs people hired me to walk, I looked like a palm tree sprouting out of a canine island. Or so one of my boyfriends said. He was forty-one; I was sixteen. He thought he had to say clever things to keep me interested because he was so old. He did.

Clients paid me five dollars extra to bathe a dog, but I'd just run it through a car wash and tip the kid a buck. I had a painted purple beauty mark. I wore my skirts up to here. Sometimes I'd take a dozen dogs to the Kung Fu triple bill. The usher let us in because I slipped him a few dollars and because I had firm fabulous thighs. The dogs sprawled on the floor, mopping up soda with their belly hair and making themselves sick on Milk Duds. One afternoon the manager offered me a hundred dollars to go to Atlantic City. No way, José. I was only twelve, for gosh sakes, even though I said I was sixteen. I was always mature for my age. And he was fat.

On warm Saturdays, when the park was filled with dads and

. . . .

daughters, I'd hitch the dogs to a little wagon and display a sign: PONY RIDES $1. When kids complained about the lack of actual ponies, I'd roll my eyes, like it was all a joke. If a dad demurred, I'd lick my lips and flip through the repertoire of coquettish mannerisms I copied from that anchorwoman on ABC. (I think she's gone on to some other job, probably in Las Vegas. Now I study Dan Rather; he smolders.) As soon as I'd loaded the wagon with skeptical children, the dogs would fan out in different directions, spilling kids all over the grass. Most dads asked for a refund and my phone number. Fat chance, Vance. One time this powdery old dame caught me hitching up her stupid schnauzer and really pitched a fit. So what? I've got the lean and leggy look for today's body-baring fashions, and she'll soon be dead.

Even before my dog-walking days, when I still lived at home, I was developing a now look: Mom insisted. Twice a year, we took the bus from our home in South Dakota to Chicago so I could gain sophistication. While we were away Daddy played poker with his pals and built elaborate scale models of historic agricultural equipment. He was a gentleman farmer; he worked for the biggest accounting firm in Pierre. Years after I left home, Mom learned that he'd been buying his replicas ready-made and having an affair with the woman who owned the hobby shop.

In Chicago Mom and I spent hours at the Metropolitan Museum of Beauty. My favorite exhibit was a collection of painful and dangerous accessories on loan from the Smithsonian Institution. A lead-shielded vitrine held an assortment of cesium eye shadows from the fifties. In a diorama a team of oxen turned a winch, tightening the stays on an antebellum corset. There was a three-hundred-and-fifty-pound ball gown, eighty yards of velvet draped on a cast-iron frame, worn at the inauguration of

· · · · · · · ·

President Taft. His diary describes "the crisp pistol-shot of ver-
tebrae bursting all during the dancing." Young and impression-
able, I found these terrifying displays thoroughly enchanting; I
yearned to become a part of it all.

But Mom said I had to finish high school, which was hypo-
critical, because every night she watched the New NBC News
Team, and they hadn't made it past junior high. Overage ex-
Zoli models—they were in their mid-twenties—they had min-
iature loudspeakers surgically implanted in their throats so they
could "read" copy written by flabby poli-sci majors with drab
lifeless hair. The program was shot with robot cameras. The
director was a genetically engineered squirrel.

At one of our weekly family meetings we settled my immediate
future. I'd live in New York City for a year, attend the Revlon
Exquisite Children's School, get a kooky gamine job, and sort
out my options.

I was walking the dogs and thinking about entering the Miss
Teen USA Pageant (Diane Sawyer won when she was my age,
and I believe Dan Rather snagged his state crown) when Rusty,
a fat little terrier that looks like a foetal pig, broke away. I hate
calling the dogs because it emphasizes one of my flaws. Here
they are: my nose is a bit off-center; my teeth are on the small
side; my voice is too high-pitched. It keeps me from being taken
seriously. I was reluctantly hollering, "Come here, Rusty, or I'll
kill you!" when Paulo Casaverde asked to take my picture.
Naked. Surrounded by dogs. I didn't know if I'd be naked or
he would, but either way it was good money.

So I had tiny teeth and a reedy voice, and when we reached
his studio, Paulo learned about my final flaw—animal feet. My
elegant legs tapered down to hard little hoofs. All my shoes had
to be altered, all my lovers warned. None of my relatives has

. . . .

unusual feet, except for Daddy, who has only nine toes. He lost one to a harvester at a farm machinery collectors convention, or so he says. Mom says his hobby-shop slut probably bit it off. Paulo said my goat feet make a charming personal trademark.

His modeling agency, Apogee, was organized into two divisions. The Beau Ideal girls were all-American beauties with long legs, big teeth, and hands the size of softball mitts. Apogee's other branch, Incroyable!!, handled madcap offbeat beauties— a languorous Moroccan girl with three firm and perfect breasts, a gorgeously proportioned Dane covered with a dense pelt of blond hair, a paroled felon (formerly a Reagan aide) with two aluminum fingers, and me. Paulo was a demanding coach, and I was willing to pay the price of beauty in pain—tighter spandex, higher heels, fewer ribs. Soon I had the whole dizzy whirl of glamour and fame and illicit drugs and thick-necked pro-sports boyfriends. And when I became the spokesmodel for John Deere Tractors there were bushel baskets of lovely money. Daddy glowed with pride and sexual confusion.

Paulo taught me to cultivate a vivid fantasy life during photo sessions. "Otherwise, you do not look erotic, merely vacant— good for snagging a rock-star husband, bad for selling spark plugs." Most of the girls think about shopping. I thought about love, even on my first job, a public service ad for the State Department. I wore six-inch heels and a SemiSilk (made in USA) teddy and held a Stinger missile. I imagined a fabulously handsome man striding out of a Fifth Avenue apartment. One of the dogs, Cupcake, mauls his leg. There's blood everywhere. I clamber into the ambulance with him, and on the way to the hospital our eyes lock. He quips, I twinkle. His wounds aren't as bad as they look, and a little club soda will clean the bloodstains off that topcoat. But he picks up an infection in the emergency room and is dead by morning. People think if you have eyes as blue as the Aegean and higher-than-high cheekbones, everything goes your way, but it doesn't always.

My first catalog work was for Lefcourt Dental Supply. They demanded that their models be over eighteen, so I told them I was. I wore Cottonette (produced in America with pride) tap pants and thought about the same man, the same horrifying fountain of arterial blood. This time skilled work by an Emergency Medical Technician (He thinks I'm a fox. I am.) saves his life. Sadly, the leg must come off. Of course, he sues. At the trial I flip for the one-legged guy's attorney: long eyelashes! He takes me and my family for every dime we've got.

For my first cover, *Pension Fund Manager*, my breasts were enhanced with SiliGel (installed by Yankee craftsmen). I imagined one of the stupid dogs drinking gray throbbing water from the Central Park reservoir. The next day he sprouts wings. The government sends a hunky toxicologist to investigate. He discovers that my hair is a shimmering cascade of sunshine framing a cameo-cute face. The winged dog, a Lab-shepherd mix, bites him. Interspecies jealousy. His arms swell to the size of sofas and he drops dead. Just as well: these brainy guys believe any girl with a perfectly pouty mouth must be a total bonehead, so it wouldn't have worked out.

During my first TV job—I ran the tote board on a telethon raising money to build prisons—I envisioned a giant of a man, rugged and austere, wandering near the Delacorte Theater, checking his trap-line. He's the manliest man I've ever seen, and I'll bet he made that fur hat himself, God knows from what. He shoots one of the dogs and eats it, but that's OK: every relationship has its period of adjustment. People assume that if you're bikini-beautiful, things fall into your lap; they do.

. . . .

I had a little liposuction to idealize my thighs before my next assignment. The surgeon asked if I'd sell whatever he vacuumed out of me to "an anonymous lover of beauty." It's not an unusual request. There's a U.S. senator who has the fat cells of ex-Rockettes massaged into his shoulders. A televangelist sautés with fat from the hips of Academy Award winners (God knows where he gets it)—fish, eggs, grilled cheese sandwiches. Like most of the girls, I'm storing it in a refrigerated vault until I'm eighteen, when I'll have the maturity to decide on a fair price, insurance against the day I'm too old to model. It's a young girl's game, modeling, and sentiment won't save me. Although I made Incroyable!!! successful enough to add a third exclamation point to its name, business, as Paulo says, is business.

The future? Who knows? Case hurrah, hurrah, I always say. Daddy thinks that the local NBC station in Pierre will shift from a single anchor to a teen-fox news team. If they do, I'm in. They'll alter my voice electronically, pushing it down among the altos. Sitting behind the news desk, I can keep my feet off-camera. I'll do a come-hither trick with my eyebrows when I talk about oil spills. And when I describe the tight money policies of the Fed, I'll let my little pink tongue play across my lips. I've got a lot to learn if I want to be a network quality journalist. People think if you have sultry, sexy Euro-curves you can get by on your looks. You can.

. . . .

SMALL
BUSINESS

For a little while I'll keep my day job managing the Kopy
King—I'm the reliable old guy among a flock of smug under-
graduate part-timers. But in the mornings before work I'll write
advertorials on spec for R. J. Reynolds while my wife, Marcie,
stirring things in the kitchen, shouts encouragement through
clouds of Wheatena steam. On weekends she'll pitch in. We'll
make a game of it, vying to compose the best offer of compensation without admitting wrongdoing; the loser washes the
dishes. We'll be the best damn voice the tobacco industry ever
had.

Then one evening I'll come home, my fingers unsmudged with
Xerox toner. I'll have gone to the bank, withdrawn our savings,
and put down first-and-last on an old garage, just big enough
to squeeze some desks between a couple of Dodge vans, the
perfect setting for our plucky struggle. There we'll refine our
ideas, making them appealing to Philip Morris. And soon an
infusion of tobacco cash will have us moving uptown to real
offices with water coolers, security passes, petty pilferage of
stationery supplies, the nasal buzz of flame-retardant carpet.

. . . .

We'll innovate like crazy, rocketing beyond the stodgy refutations cranked out by the Tobacco Institute. Their sound bites will seem like big, dumb radio tubes as we devise smaller and smaller denial units of dazzling efficiency—infomorsels, quotelettes, minidemurrals. We'll develop the reliable deniability that can turn any surgeon general into a stooge. A small entrepreneurial operation, we'll be agile enough to respond to rapidly changing market conditions just in case market conditions ever do change. Like say people stop smoking and start sprinkling tobacco on their cereal to get more fiber. We'll adapt over the weekend, but a bloated dinosaur like the Tobacco Institute will keep operating on the old assumptions for months. Years.

The Tobacco Institute is strictly defensive—reacting, refuting, rebutting: I want to attack. I'll advertise in literary quarterlies, soliciting applications for Poet Laureate of the Tobacco Industry, a lucrative post whose sole duty will be creating names for future brands of cigarettes. I anticipate an avalanche of responses—Serenity Wisps, Studs, Honey Haze Longs, Mameluke Spindrifts, Permafrost Ethereals.

Imagine the research projects we can underwrite once we tap that vast Liggett and Meyers bank account! A professor at the community college has a monkey that smokes Newports. The monkey is eighty-three years old; smoking has preserved him in some way connected to amino acids. Whenever the monkey gets the flu, the mentholated smoke dries out his lungs; his colds never last more than three hours. Could smoking be a cure for the common (monkey) cold? Further research surely is called for.

Or not. I have my moments of doubt. Sad fact: 50 percent of first businesses fail. (And first marriages, Marcie reminds me, but we've been durable enough to withstand two and a half

. . . .

years of bliss.) And, oh, the heartbreak of the new empty restaurant. Peer through the window at linens so white the tables
seem to be covered with plaster of paris. By next year it will be
a New-Laundromat-Coming-Soon. Well, that just means I must
work hard and plan ahead. I've heard about a guy who can
arrange for a flash flood to wipe out assets you didn't realize
you had. First thing I'll do is put in for federal flood insurance.

Question: should we smoke around the office? These big cor-
porations demand sincerity, brand loyalty, team spirit, that sort
of stuff. What if they spot-checked us to see if we would-be
spokesmen were true tobacco fanciers? To be on the safe side,
maybe we should keep a jar of smoker's urine in the refrigerator.

I'll sign us up for Lobbyist League softball. Picture it: the park
is cool and green, the Asbestos Board is battering the Lead Smelt-
ers Council in the adjacent field, and the Leaky Canisters of
Suspected Carcinogens Association blimp is circling overhead,
rectifying public perceptions. After our game we'll go out for
beer and shoptalk with our vanquished colleagues from the Liquor, Guns, and Dirt Bikes Committee. Thousands of American
families rely on the production and sale of liquor, guns, and dirt
bikes for their livelihood.

"There are two sides to every story," someone will say. "Our
job is to put the side of an incredibly profitable industry before
the public, who, if they disagree, can always write their congressman. It's a free country. I'm entitled to my opinion. You're
not my mother. I'm rubber and you're glue: anything you say
bounces off me and sticks to you.

"No one believes that a magazine ad can get a kid to chug
half a dozen allegedly tainted wine coolers, strap on an easily
concealed handgun, and zigzag through traffic on a motorcycle
purported to be uncontrollable even at low speed. Can't be done.

. . . .

All our ads do is suggest that an adult might like to sample a new brand of beverage, a different model firearm, another recreational vehicle. Basically, we're a consumer information service."

I'll nod affably and add, "Hey, you can't blame an entire industry for the irresponsible actions of a few death-susceptible individuals."

During batting practice, between innings, icing down an injury, I'll hear whispers of contingency plans for the tobacco industry in the post-cigarette era. A Virginia printer works around the clock running off copies of *Cooking with Tobacco, Cajun Style*: it might be by Paul Prudhomme. In North Carolina there's a carbon steel locker jammed with sweaters and tires made of durable, attractive Tobalon fiber. A Kentucky warehouse holds hundreds of cans of meaty-tasting Tobacat pet food.

There may be darker doings. Suppose an aerobics star collapses on her own TV show, her arteries clogged with tropical oils. What if an inspiring over-forty biathlete drops dead in mid-meet, his lung tissue as brittle as coral? Imagine the reaction if the respected physician-author of *Wellness* achieves critical mass on the *Today* show, threatening a melt-down perilously near to Jane Pauley's hair. Pro-health pressure groups would be undermined; the smokers' rights movement would be strengthened. Can such things be left to chance? Does a multibillion-dollar industry expect its Institute to do no more than run obfuscating ads in *USA Today*?

In the shift to a global service economy, only the most technologically sophisticated will thrive. My Tobacco Information Bureau will have the best beepers, the fastest fax, full-duplex hands-free cellular car phones, stylish Armani jackets lined with bullet-stopping Kevlar. It will be equipped with the user-

. . . .

friendliest desktop publishing systems, mounted on railroad cars in the Mojave Desert. Ceaselessly shuttling from prestigious location to prestigious location, we will elude our competitors and befuddle misguided antismoking absolutists. They won't be able to find us, let alone counter our deftly assembled sophistries. I'll tell you this, pal: if I were the Tobacco Institute, I'd be checking my rearview mirror.

THE
NEW FIRST
LADY

Before the New First Lady's motorcade can enter the Bel Mar Galleria, her support crew must clear a path through the foam cups and burger boxes that surge and eddy across the parking lot. In places the drifts are eight feet high. Mall gangs—punks and stoners—have been overturning dumpsters again. "They get the idea from that song 'Trash Run Free; Why Can't Me,' " says the New First Lady. She wants it purged from the discount rack at Tower Records as part of her "Let 'Em Pay List Price" pro-family campaign. Six small electric snowplows, Hondas, trundle in formation through the lot, their drivers wearing the cheerful orange-and-green uniform of the Mall Police. The going is slow, especially where foam packing nodules have been sprayed with lighter fluid and set afire. Smoke cuts visibility; the gas masks are cumbersome. The New First Lady may be late for the opening ceremony, when kids come forward, turn in their parents for running sex cassettes on the VCR, and receive a Smut-Buster badge. The delay and the smoldering styrene fumes seeping into the car are making her jittery, but she does

. . . .

THE NEW FIRST LADY

not falter in her determination to enter the mall. "No American must be denied that most reliable way to gain a sense of accomplishment—participating in our economy on the demand side," she says.

She is the guest of the General William C. Westmoreland Retirement Center's amateur orchestra, the Jolly Pals. These jaunty graybeards play country favorites and commercial jingles on small off-brand electronic keyboards, instruments they grew to love once they overcame their fear of electric shock. Now the sprightly seniors savor their ability to sound like a banjo or a fiddle or a clog dancer on a tin roof. "Sure I'm chipper," admits Elsie Bauman. "Rage takes cash. My social security check barely covers crusty-but-lovable." Her hands are swathed in bandages where a carelessly wired C-sharp key gave her a bad electrical burn.

This afternoon the Jolly Pals will play "We Are All Old," an anthem of caring composed by top pop stars enlisted by the New First Lady to discharge the community service portion of their plea bargains. Helping gerio-Americans is deeply important to her. She induced many big-time rockers to join hands for the video. Its proceeds will go toward making us feel good about loving some feelings of compassion for ourselves and others. Projects like this one are what the New First Lady calls responsible rebellion in a commercially viable context consistent with Christian living. "This isn't political," she insists. "It's just people getting together to do things for people." She mentions the charity ball and mink war that paid for resurfacing the off-ramps of I-78. Of course one night of blood and dancing can't do everything. Additional funding came from the big sing-athon, "We Are All Long-Haul Truckers." Such selflessness won't go unnoticed at the next Rock'n'Roast Trophy Dinner,

. . . .

particularly when it's time to present the Merrill Lynch Humanitarian Award.

These nimble baldpates are only one concern of the New First Lady; she has dozens of others. Her initial issue, back when the Policy Team first began to reformulate her, was the Very Young, and she continues to demand aggressive action on missing children, although she sometimes muddles the particulars. Are there too many missing children or too few? Should government do more, or ought this be left to the private sector where children could be lost (found?) more efficiently? Should their photographs appear on more packages, perhaps on huge wooden crates, ambiguously stenciled "machine parts," destined for the Central American combat zones after a swoop through several Mideast nations? This worthwhile volunteer effort was financed by the danceable anthem "We Are All Missing."

Currently her Issues Analysis Team is urging her to emphasize a new caring area. She is to be passionately devoted, with an appropriate coefficient of modesty, to medical research, in particular the fight against infectious pseudomnesia. A degenerative mental disorder, pseudomnesia is not the loss of recall but, rather, the accretion of false memories. Those afflicted have vivid recollections of things that never happened; true and false memories become indistinguishable. Patricia, a pseudomnesia sufferer, says she remembers Niagara Falls. Her doctor, a brusque tough-love healer, dismisses this possibility. "She remembers a cornball romantic anecdote from a post-honeymoon cousin, or a photo in the *World Book* glimpsed during the fourth grade when she should have been doing math, or that Marilyn Monroe movie. Or maybe, just maybe," he grudgingly concedes, "she has that rarest of conditions, a pure retrospective hallucination."

Cause? Unknown. Most research money goes to the virolo-

. . . .

gists. They've got the most promising initial results, the most photogenic research scientists, the sleekest graphics on their multipage fund-raising mailer with many computer inserts of the recipient's name ("Yes, Recipient, thanks to the efforts of people like you, Recipient, we can now do various important . . ."). And they have the least likelihood of pinpointing a cause that will lead to product liability suits, criminal indictments, loss of Senate seats. In other labs, impressive statistical data—albeit the kind that can be shrugged off as coincidence by well-coiffed corporate spokesmen—are being assembled by the Environmental Factors Team. They point to thousands of postwar tract houses hastily erected for returning troops and fecund GI brides, on the sites of abandoned cigarette-filter factories or over shimmering pools of diet-soda prototypes, casually covered with sand and gravel. "But you can't be scientifically certain," says the man from the Heritage Foundation, lighting another low-tar. "Research must continue unfettered by government regulation, untainted by government funds. Money will come from that soul-stirring hymn of helping, 'We Are All Neurally Befuddled,' now available on compact disc."

As long as its cause is unknown, pseudomnesia must be considered a communicable disease. The New First Lady fears contagion, but she appears at the galleria, taking what preventive measures she can, her breathing tubes barely apparent beneath her flounces and shoulder pads. Certain parts of her body have been perma-dipped in latex. A padded titanium case in the trunk of her limo holds a thermos of her own blood plus smaller canisters of six other bodily fluids. She does not lack courage. As a Senate wife, she continued to swaddle herself in fur throughout the "Days of Tooth and Claw"—violent outbursts by the Animal Liberation Army. Even in her former mode, while still

. . . .

in thrall to her Republican predecessors, her primary duty merely to display a flair for stylish acquisition, she was dauntless. Holding her Visa card aloft like a sword, she didn't panic but continued to try on Oscar de la Renta gowns amid the co-op riots, while all around her SWAT teams battled through Trumptown, a few dozen shanties protesters had built in Saks.

Today's galleria appearance is a triumph, luring many shoppers to linger for three or four minutes before drifting back to the Shirt Bunker, with its cheerful khaki-clad clerks and wacky anti-Basque novelty items. But midway through her speech, just before she is to review the Remorseful Teens and Their Children Drill Team, something happens. The New First Lady rambles on about Wrigley Field in 1968. "Student radicals had dug tunnels beneath the pitcher's mound," she recalls, "and packed them with explosives, set to detonate when Kate Smith hit that vexing high note in our national anthem. If Mayor Daley hadn't jumped into his Mole-Car and burrowed . . ." The crowd looks confused, the Jolly Pals are spooked. Curious consumers watch her spiral to the floor in a surprisingly graceful faint; in her preteens she studied ballet, and she still has the powerful thighs and visible ribs of a classical dancer. Uzis drawn, Secret Service agents rush her to the limousine as the Mall Police lob Tear Gas Plus into the crowd. (Just like the song in the commercial: "Tough on rioters, tender on gentle fabrics.") The P.A. system commands: "Return to your purchasing. There is nothing for you here. Resume shopping immediately." To avoid pursuit, the limo driver flings handfuls of perfume-sample packets out of the sunroof, like chum to a school of bluefish.

For nearly a week no diagnosis comes from the White House, only bland denials that the New First Lady had contracted pseudomnesia. Eventually the official explanation of the episode—

. . . .

exhaustion—is announced on beautifully embossed ivory cards, postage paid by the New First Lady's booster group, participants in the Adopt a Quasi–Government Official program.

To quiet the rumors, the New First Lady agrees to be interviewed on a Barbara Walters Special, along with a powerful intellectual, a potential saint, and a woman with fabulous cheekbones. "Where would you place yourself on this continuum?" Barbara asks.

"Well . . ." the New First Lady looks bemused.

"Suppose the worst happened, and you lost your wonderful vibrancy, and—forgive me for asking anything upsetting—you found you had—God forbid!—pseudomnesia. Would you feel different about the Stop and Sample laws or the CheekScraper or the rest of your husband's Omnibus Wellness Program?"

"No. Not even if I were ordered to live in one of the Healthvilles in Nevada. My position would be unchanged."

It was a stirring assertion, and it sent Americans racing to record stores for "We Are All the New First Lady." Its melody is haunting and familiar. The New First Lady suspects that she has heard it—somewhere—before.

THE MOM
SQUAD

By order of the governor exercised under the authority of the Emergency Powers Act, the Bureau of Missing Persons established a new elite division, the Mom Squad. Its mission: locate and return to their families the growing army of runaway moms.
> —*From orientation lecture, Police Academy,*
> *Mom Squad Candidates School*

WE ALWAYS GET OUR MOM
> —*plaque over doorway, Mom Squad HQ*

The training at the Academy was great, especially the Mom Recognition Patterns. Like last week, I was on routine mom-spotting patrol at the Food Queen. One of the things they taught us is to spot them at the check-out line. Look for a lot of salad stuff, especially unusual greens and avocados, things that guys and kids don't like. Also unflavored yogurt and small pieces of lean meat, like veal chops.
> —*Patrolman Gus Swindon, M.S.*

. . . .

The public has been super-cooperative. When I flip on the Klaxon, everybody recognizes it as the "Mom Spotted" signal. Some phone the station for backup, some let us commandeer their cars. And there hasn't been a single lawsuit against the squad from a civilian hit by a stray round.

—*Sgt. Mike Nachako, M.S.*

I remember coming home from practice and not smelling brownies. I was scared.

—*Stanley Bobbinski, age 11*

I yelled, "Mom, did you iron my shirt?" But she didn't answer. I figured she was just emptying the garbage or something, so I went into the den to watch TV.

—*Chuck Bobbinski, age 17*

Look, I'm just a kid. I don't think I should have to spend my nights hemming a lot of stuff. I want to go out on dates like other girls. It's not fair. I hate her for this.

—*Dagmar Bobbinski, age 14*

Everybody says, "Don't blame yourself, Rob. You're a good husband." I dunno. Maybe if I'd paid a little more attention to her, if I'd taken the time to say, "Nice job waxin' the floor, hon." If, if, if. Well, if she's out there somewhere reading this, I just want to say, "Honey, the kids and I miss you. We need you. Please come home."

—*Robert Bobbinski, age 42*

The real victims are the families they leave behind. It's oh so stylish to talk about the romance of moms on the run, but we

. . . .

forget that for each Nan Bobbinski out there buying small portions of lean meat, there's a Bobbinski family back home: hurt, frightened, bewildered.

—*Dr. Karl Manheim, psychiatrist*

The doctors worked up what we call a "Psychological Profile" of the PRM, Potential Runaway Mom. She's got what they call DMC—Diminished Maternal Capacity. That's what we watch for. Heck, to tell you the truth, I wish I was back on burglary.

—*Patrolman Peter Lemberg, M.S.*

What gets me isn't how many make a break for it, but how few. In their shoes, pal, I'd be long gone, I can tell you.

—*Lt. Alec Barstow, M.S.*

My first job right out of law school was defending these gals. I specialized in maternity law at State/Poly. These moms, they could break your heart, the stories they tell. Someone's got to help them, and I wouldn't hold my breath waiting for *Redbook* or Procter & Gamble or the Republican National Committee to kick in any serious dough to the Moms Defense Fund. And you can kiss off the state legislature, for sure.

—*Della Spivak, Atty.*

She said she was going to the corner to buy some new laundry products to really get at those stains. That was in October of '83, and I haven't seen her since.

—*Kelly Chisinau, abandoned dad*

It is so much for me to be learning of your modern police methods and also of your American customs. I am often being per-

. . . .

plexed by your ways. For instance, you are permitting your moms to drive the cars and to attend the extension-school classes and to read the *Newsweek* magazine and to be swimming in the ocean with the men. These things we do not allow in my country. I have much to learn.

—*Sgt. Anwar Akim, on loan from Riyadh PD*

This one time, I was on foot patrol at Woolworth's, and I had a runaway mom spotted. You could tell. Maybe it was the way she ignored men's underwear and school supplies and . . . well, I don't know exactly. You develop an instinct. Anyhow, I go to ID her, and she pulls out this little .25 caliber and starts blasting. Holy cow! You'd think they'd realize that we only want to help them. Right now, regulations let us draw our side arms only if a mom fires first. Most guys want to see that changed. In fact, most of the guys want to carry shotguns.

—*Det. Richard Eiger, M.S.*

Look, I don't want to be known as the first woman on the Mom Squad. I'm not a libber or anything. I'm just another cop trying to do a job.

—*Det. Melissa Teche, M.S.*

The United States is a signatory of the Damascus Accords, which specify conventions for the repatriation of fugitive moms. However, the Bureau does not believe that the moms are part of any international organization. Frankly, they aren't organized at all. Most of these moms have no idea where they'll go or what they'll do. Your typical runaway just gets fed up one day and bolts. It's kind of sad when you think about it—millions of tuna-noodle

. . . .

casseroles burnt to a crisp while around the world children go to bed hungry.

—*Agent Douglas Wicklow, FBI*

My committee will recommend extending the Mom Recovery and Detention Act to cover anyone more than ten weeks pregnant. I'm aware of the emotional debate we can expect, but let's not lose sight of the larger issue: our family maintenance law is a mess, a hodgepodge of regulations that vary wildly from state to state. For example, right now the FBI can enter a case only if a mom crosses a state line or if her husband is engaged in interstate commerce. I say it's time for a tough National Family Code to bring order out of this chaos.

—*Congressman Claude Riga (R, Utah)*

NECESSITY FOR THE MOTHER IS DETENTION
—*graffito, block 17, Strayhorn Maternal Detention Facility*

Forget what you see on TV. They make it seem like the most exciting thing going is to spend a night in a patrol car with the Mom Squad. Well, it's not. It's boring and it's routine. Mostly what you do is drive around and complain to your partner about married life, or maybe you talk about baseball. You cruise the neighborhood and you keep your eyes open, and in the back of your mind you're always thinking—maybe the next mom we tag will be carrying a Kalashnikov AK-47 assault rifle. Some excitement, huh? Not quite what they do on "Sgt. Danvers, M.S.," is it? You know, my kids watch that program every week; they wouldn't miss it. I hate that damn show.

—*Patrolman Thomas Arafuro, M.S.*

. . . .

RADIO DOCTOR

ON THE AIR

"Moving up to sixty-four springlike degrees here on all-talk Fifty-Five, your information station, and let's take another call. 'Radio Doctor.' You're on the air."

"Is this 'Radio Doctor'?"

"You're on the air, sir. Turn your radio down."

"I'm on the air?"

"That's right. You're on 'Radio Doctor.' Where does it hurt?"

"First let me say that we listen to you all the time here at Herbst Brake Linings, and we love the show."

"Well, thanks very much. Smile twice and call me in the morning. Now, can you describe your symptoms?"

"I think it's my hemoglobin. Can you say hemoglobin on the radio?"

"The only thing you can't say on this show is 'malpractice suit.' But I don't think you can feel your hemoglobin. Tell me a little more."

. . . .

"I'm kind of uncomfortable talking about it to a woman. Where's the regular doctor?"

"Dr. Nussman is at a sports-medicine conference in Cancun; I'm taking his patients for a few days. There's no reason to be embarrassed; I've heard hundreds of penises described since I started broadcasting."

"You're right. It is my penis, but it doesn't exactly hurt; it's more of a throbbing whenever—"

"Hold that for just a moment, OK? We've got to do a commercial, but we'll be back in ninety seconds for more with— what's your name?"

"Frank."

"—Frank's penis, right after this word from the nice folks at the Meadowsoft Bedding Center. Meadowsoft: for the rest of your life."

During the commercial, Dr. Ellen Kaplan slips off her headphones and sips a decaf. Dr. Nussman has a bicycle horn mounted on the edge of the table; he gives it a congratulatory squeeze whenever he makes a particularly apt remark. Tilting it up toward the ceiling, Ellen pours the rest of her coffee into its open end.

SELF-IMPROVEMENT

The language of jovial blather required on "Radio Doctor" was foreign to Ellen, so the station hired a consultant to help her. "Listeners will like you, Ellen, if you're cheerful and positive," explained Brian Massey. Only nineteen, he owns a company that programs sixty-four radio stations around the country. Being professionally in tune with the times has made Brian a teenage millionaire; he has a video game in his bathroom. Most of the sentences he speaks to Ellen include her name. "Up is the national direction, Ellen, and optimism is the national mood." Brian sees a glimmer of distaste roll across Ellen's face, like the headlights of a passing car across a bedroom wall. "Hey. I get paid whether you take my advice or not. So go be a foul-mouthed sociopath. I've sent stations down that road and got great numbers, but, baby, you're no Morton Downey. So if you want an audience, you'd better start thinking perky and dapper and peppy."

She does, picturing three cartoon mice, their names stenciled onto their brightly colored T-shirts: Perky, Dapper, Peppy. Foam flecks the corners of Perky's snout as he turns to Dapper. "Die, vermin, die," snarls Perky, plunging his fangs into Dapper's throat and clawing at his underbelly. Blood spatters Peppy's fur as he prances gleefully a few feet away. Soon his two rivals will be wounded and weak, and he'll leap in and finish them both off.

"It's not easy for me, Brian," Ellen says, "but I'm going to try."

A PREVIOUS PROGRAM

Ellen was free to fill in at "Radio Doctor" because her own show had just been canceled. "What's Up Down There" with Dr. Ellen Kaplan, your gynecologist of the air, demonstrated the station's commitment to women's concerns. It followed "Jock Beat," hosted by Kyle Ermold, a high-school football coach. An unathletic child who'd been tormented by her better-coordinated classmates, Ellen detested Kyle and thought of "Jock Beat" as remedial radio for slow listeners. She often sang to herself as she walked down the corridor past the workmen ripping out the

. . . .

asbestos insulation: "Baby baby, can't you hear my jock beat? Baby baby, can't you hear my jock beat?"

Fearing a sex discrimination suit, the station gave plenty of promotional support to "What's Up Down There." Ellen's face appeared on the side of city buses as the queen of hearts in a poker hand made up of the station's top personalities; within a week the bus fleet became a rolling thesaurus of spray-painted genital synonyms. There were newspaper ads and TV spots. When Ellen aired a special series, the station ordered new jingles: "Hey! It's PMS Week on Radio 55."

Her show ran from four to six in the afternoon, drive time, so most of her listeners were in their cars heading home from work. She felt like an odd combination of Ob-Gyn specialist and driving instructor: right there, that's your cervix, and that long thing is your turn signal. Ellen worried that some listener, alert for symptoms, would shift her attention from the road to her lap, and rear-end the car in front of her. "I swear, Officer, it darted out in front of me. I think it was a yeast infection."

A PROFESSIONAL SETBACK

"It's not politics, El, OK?" Doug Hewett, the station manager, was using his best straight-from-the-shoulder style. Ellen was sure he'd rehearsed this speech in the men's room mirror. "It's ratings. Our listeners are vaginally bored. Secretions, discharges —let's put them behind us. 'What's Up Down There' is dead, but Dr. Ellen Kaplan is very much alive. We're working on several projects for you, and we want your input. Think about a program you'd like to do."

As Hewett chattered on, Ellen thought about a call-in show she'd like to try. ". . . Mistress Helga. You're on the air, you miserable worm."

. . . .

"Oh, Mistress Helga, I've been very bad, and I must be punished."

"Silence! I alone decide who must be punished . . . and how."

A moist whimper came over the phone.

"You disgust me. First, turn your radio down."

More whimpering, and some scurrying.

"Now we can begin."

HER FIRST RADIO SHOW

Ellen joined the station when it was converting to an all-talk format. Her first show was called "Rock in Hell: The Power Hour." She played records—Metallica, Whitesnake, Wasp. It was a temporary assignment until the changeover was completed. A novice, she stuck close to the scripted material, saying, "It's coming up on eight twenty-five, and it's going to burn!" and "Taste the boot!" She was issued petty cash and sent to buy a leather dress, a studded glove, and a dog collar. "Save the receipts," Doug Hewett reminded her. The glove made it easier to open jars. She put the collar on her dog, Zeno. But she thought she looked great in the dress. It was curiously satisfying to know that if she wanted to date fourteen-year-old boys, she could take her pick. These days she wasn't dating anyone. Not seriously. Not anyone who wasn't a jerk.

BAD SEX

Ellen lazes in the bath, drinking a glass of wine and not concentrating on her book. Zeno is curled up by the sink. Ellen wonders, Should I henna my hair? Go back to shaving under my arms? She thinks, All happy sex is alike, but each night of unhappy sex is miserable in its own way.

. . . .

93

Andy Drexler. He thought I was fat. I couldn't stop thinking: flabby thighs, flabby thighs.

Elliot Berman. Brief, jangling, confusing—like your first game of PacMan. Not as noisy.

Mark Jennings. Tentative. It made me nervous. He couldn't pick a restaurant; that should have tipped me off.

Matt Trantino. He couldn't get over my outearning him.

Tom Cseszlow. He was drunk.

Kenny Talbert. I was drunk.

Phil Boyer. Talk about selfish!

David Adler. I have no idea. It was perfect on paper, but nothing was happening.

Ellen sips her wine. Zeno stretches and drinks some water out of the toilet.

Norman Mailer. Oddly misinformed.

Mikhail Baryshnikov. Great to look at but not much fun to do, like photographs of a bad vacation.

Keith Hernandez. Too intense.

Bruce Springsteen. Probably my fault. I kept thinking: model/actress/wife.

Sigourney Weaver. I'll think about it later.

Henry Kissinger. Grotesque and freakish, of course. But I hid my disgust so he'd sleep, and I could fetch the stiletto from my purse. Knee him awake. Remind him of the Cambodian invasion. Slip the knife between his ribs. Did I clean everything up? Fingerprints on the bathroom mirror? Did the doorman spot me? The cab driver—he'll remember me! Easy. Don't panic. Thousands of people wanted to see the bastard dead, most with stronger motives than mine. Everything will be all right. Stay calm. Act natural. Stick to your usual routine.

Ellen smiles, stands up, and reaches for her robe.

. . . .

BAD OFFERS

Before she joined the station Ellen had vague feelings of anxiety whenever she made her rounds at the hospital. She resented certain colleagues, dreaded the future, seldom slept through the night. She wondered if these feelings were work-related; she never looked for another job. Doug Hewett had seen her interviewed on local news, either during the soup-tampering scare or the night the seventy-one homeless guys froze to death; he wasn't sure which. He was impressed by her self-assurance and rich contralto. Ellen agreed to talk to him because she loved bad offers: you feel desirable when you receive them and virtuous when you turn them down.

"Basically," said Hewett, "it's what you're doing now, only with an audience."

Ellen imagines "Radio Emergency Room." Clambering over a fence, a beery hunter puts a bullet through his thigh. He turns on his radio and spins the dial until he hears his symptoms described on the air. It could be weeks.

"Not in the sense of bleeding and screaming," Doug went on, "more of a people thing. Look, what can't you get anyone to do?"

Oh dear, she thought, it's going to be about older men and oral sex. "I don't know, Doug. Paint my apartment? Hook up my VCR?"

"A sense of humor—very radiogenic. OK. Here it is: families. The social center of the late eighties. 'Father Knows Best,' 'Ozzie and Harriet,' and the big one, 'Marcus Welby, M.D.' See what I'm getting at?"

For a panicky moment, Ellen thought he was proposing mar-

. . . .

riage and, more frightening, she realized she was considering it. Not favorably, but still . . .

"House calls! That's what you can't get, and that's what we'll call your show. A doorbell rings, bing-bong, muted and nostalgic. Who is it? It's you, offering comfortable authority-figure advice to a postfeminist wife taking a few years off from her challenging career to stay in her lovely home and raise her fascinating children, who are sick as dogs, moaning like mules, puking all over the couch. And Mom, for all her MBAs, is going nuts. A savvy analysis of the Euro-bond market won't help her now. What does she do? Break down? Crack up? No! She clicks on the radio and turns to her trusted family physician. And you tell her—"

"I tell her that infanticide was accepted by history's most advanced civilizations, the ancient Athenians, for instance."

Six weeks later, Ellen left the hospital and came to work at Radio-55.

ROSE KAPLAN

When Ellen quit the hospital, no one felt worse than her mother, Rose, and when Ellen started at the station, no one was more encouraging. Rose relished a chance to display enthusiasm for other people's lives. She had dozens of suggestions that made Ellen quiver with irritation. "That Diane Sawyer did quite a job on '60 Minutes,' " Rose observed. "Why not call her up? Maybe the two of you could do something together."

Whenever Ellen was assigned to a new show, her mother would call, exercising what she thought was a gift for mimicry. During "What's Up Down There," Rose phoned almost daily as one or another great lady of the American musical theater.

Ethel Merman complained about cramps. Someone in a revival of *Brigadoon* had an unusually copious flow. Sprinkling her conversation with putative drug references, Rose tried again and again to win a pair of Iron Maiden tickets on the Power Hour, but the answer to the trivia question was never Artie Shaw.

One night when Ellen was lying on the couch reading, she thought about Rose ringing the doorbell.

"Oh hi, Ma," Ellen said, determined to show no annoyance. "What's up?"

"Ellen, I met the nicest guy at the bus terminal, and I told him all about you."

"Ma! What did you do that for? I don't want you fixing me up with any more guys."

"Don't be rude, sweetheart. He's right outside. Ellen. I'd like you to meet Richard Starkweather."

Ellen could see that it wasn't actually Richard Starkweather. This guy was much too cute. It was Martin Sheen.

"Listen, Richard, you look like a nice guy," Ellen said, "but I can't do this. My mother gets a little carried away. I hope you understand."

"Heck, Ellen, don't give it another thought. I'd be happy to blow your mom's head off for you."

Starkweather raised his shotgun and pumped round after round into Mrs. Kaplan.

"Thanks, Dick," Ellen said. "As long as you're here, how about if I open a bottle of wine?'

"Call me Marty."

The phone rang just as Ellen reached a particularly engrossing part of her book. She didn't doubt for a second that it was her mother.

. . . .

BACK ON THE AIR

". . . up a degree in the last hour to sixty-five, and let's go to the phones." Ellen sees that all five lines are lit up. She thinks, I should pick up some Lean Cuisine on the way home. Maybe Glazed Chicken. She says, " 'Radio Doctor.' You're on the air."

MAN-
SHARING

ONE APPROACH TO THE SHORTAGE OF MEN IS SHARING

—headline, *New York Times*

When Jeannine Kagle, vice president and director of marketing
for a large California winery, heard that her boyfriend was
going condo, she was distraught. A year later, she's delighted.
"It's time-sharing that's made the difference," Kagle smiled
from the seat of her company jet. "My career always came first
with me, and how much was I actually seeing him? A lot less
than you'd think. Now I get Jack one weekend a month plus
two weeks in the summer, and it's terrific. I save a bundle on
the upkeep and I'm still accumulating equity; the tax advantages
are obvious."

For some it was efficiency, for others the man shortage, but
for Allison Esterhause, a New York City bond trader, it was an
investment opportunity. "When Malcolm went co-op," she recalls, "I was able to pick him up at the insider price—we'd been

· · · · · · · ·

99

dating for more than a year—about fifty percent of his market value on a noneviction plan. And I flipped him immediately. I made fifty-five K on him, just over the weekend. It was the first time I'd made that much that fast, and there were no fees or commissions. With that kind of capital, I could easily afford a new boyfriend in a better neighborhood, one with a view."

As more and more executives discover the advantages of applying their professional skills to their personal lives, new companies are emerging to cater to their needs. Pamela Markham is a Senior VP at Mantech Associates, a firm that manages time-shared boyfriends and locates undervalued men about to go co-op. She notes, "We've gotten our clients in on the ground floor of some terrific guys—handsome, educated, charming, really presentable men that you can bring to dinner with your CEO and not be embarrassed."

Naturally, Markham finds interest rates to be a constant concern. "Absolutely. A lot of these guys are interested only in themselves—windbags and blowhards! But if you can find a fellow who is even moderately attentive to his partner's needs, and of course a bank that will provide the financing—anything under eleven percent these days—well, you're looking at impressive upside potential."

It was a happy accident that propelled investment banker Stephanie Ashforth into this volatile new field: "I was having one of those conversations with a woman I knew only professionally, after squash at the Athletic Club. We both were complaining about the men we were involved with, and our complaints were so similar—lack of commitment, immaturity, the sex thing. Then it hit us: we were talking about the same guy. We were each other's other woman!

"After that, it was just a matter of our lawyers sitting down

. . . .

and hammering out the details: scheduling, maintenance, liability insurance—you know, in case someone breaks him, who
covers the repair bills? And now my tax consultant tells me she
can work out a great depreciation scheme on Philip—once they
hit fifty, these men can just fall apart, you know. With what I
save, I'll be able to pick up a little young one to use around town
when I can't get away for the weekend."

Productivity gains, an unexpected by-product, have been
spectacular, reports Beryl Kramer. "With my professional ob-
ligations, I was spending very little time with Murph. I'd say
I was running him at no more than 30 percent of capacity. He'd
squander these huge blocks of downtime watching football on
TV. A total waste. Now, thanks to the time-sharing plan I've
established with a few other execs, we've got him up to 73
percent of capacity. What a saving! Your fixed costs are there
anyway—shoes, beer, dental—but your output skyrockets.
Our goal is to get him up to 90 percent by the end of the next
fiscal year. We might look for a new limited partner, or we
might go public with him. We'll hash it out between sessions
at the IMF next month; all the owners will be there, a happy
coincidence. Murph? Oh, we'll put him in the shop for routine
maintenance."

Margaret Durning, a Kansas City commodities trader, is
seeing a very attractive man on a sale and lease-back arrangement. She transferred his title to the Lamarado Development
Company and now rents him for weekends and holidays with
an option to reclaim him in five years at half his replacement
value. "The sale provided an infusion of funds that really bailed
me out of a cash-flow bind," Durning notes, "and it provided
Lamarado with some sweet tax write-offs. It's the kind of in-
novative, mutually beneficial response that makes you feel great

· · · · · · · ·

about American management. Let me tell you, the Japanese haven't gotten into this at all. They're still fumbling around with antiquated concepts. It's like the 1950s; I think they still go steady. We're way out in front on this thing. It makes you proud to be an American and an MBA."

. . . .

COMMUTER
REPORT

AMTRAK TRAINS

Carol:
Crossword puzzle, *Times* of London, in pen.

Lou:
Even harder crossword puzzle, *Post* of Jerusalem, in Hebrew.
Hopes Carol will notice. She does. Thinks he's a cluck.

Barb:
Part of bridge foursome. A terrific player and a swell gal, but
not seeing anyone seriously. (Wishes she were.)

Bette:
See above. Only an average player, but makes amusing catty
remarks. Laments the President's response to the savings and
loan crisis.

. . . .

Larry:
See above. Subpar player, but Barb finds him attractive, so she tosses a few tricks his way, then hates herself for playing dumb.

Lance:
See above. Terrible player and blowhard. The other three derive endless pleasure from beating someone so fatuous, self-satisfied, and blond.

Andrea:
Determined to avoid discussion of Amazon deforestation. Wants more sex and a piece of chocolate cake.

Chip:
Will be on later train: still at the office. And why not? He's single, no girlfriend, no close pals, nothing to go home to except an expensive slab of meat tossed into the broiler, and the sports channel on cable. He might as well throw himself into his work or out of a tenth-story window.

EXPRESSWAYS

Mal:
Thinking of transferring his savings to a tax-free bond fund and his kids to a boarding school in another state. Wants to lose about fifteen pounds.

Bill:
His new sofa was delivered this afternoon, and he's eager to get home and sit on it. Bill's in for a disappointment: it's the wrong

. . . .

color, more rust than maroon. Fears that America may already have ceded high-definition TV to the Japanese.

Mike:
Cruising right along and feeling fine. Derives enormous satisfaction from his wide tires, the flaming mythical-bird decal on his hood, the illicit drugs in his glove compartment, and the extramarital affair he's carrying on during his lunch hour. (Is in the dark about his wife's affair.)

Nancy:
Practices with French language-lesson tapes while driving: doesn't believe in wasting time. Keeps track of her mileage. Supports the tight-money policies of the Federal Reserve.

Fran:
Muses on love, real estate, proliferation of chemical weapons. Might upgrade her car stereo.

BRIDGES AND TUNNELS

Everyone grumbles about the traffic and the poor condition of the road surface. Everyone is preoccupied with his own petty concerns except Helen who is thinking of others, but nothing flattering.

SURFACE ROADS

Liz:
Ponders the struggle for Estonian independence. Thinks she may have an unpleasant but not life-threatening sexually trans-

. . . .

mitted disease. Speculates about where she got it and whom she'd like to give it to. (Actually, it's just a rash.)

Stu:
Just came up with a great advertising slogan for Jell-O. He's a broker, but continues to file these schemes at the office. You never know.

Skip:
Wearing brightly colored bikini underwear his wife gave him. Can't decide if he's pleased or embarrassed. Has passing thought about deployment of S.D.I.

Mavis:
Contemplates buying a bustier and a .357 Magnum. Makes mental note to pick up a quart of skim milk on her way home.

SUBWAYS

Lisa:
Running late because she took a long lunch with an old boyfriend. Listens to a Dylan tape on her Walkman. Has an unexpected pang of sadness for poor Brian Jones; he really was the most creative one. Feels surprisingly nostalgic for mind-altering chemicals. Wonders how, after Woodstock, she ended up in corporate law.

Anne:
Just stares into middle distance.

Tony:
Wonders if the microchip in his new oven really started the dinner all by itself. (It did.) Is glad to be gay.

. . . .

Leo:
Mentally undresses the most attractive passengers, then mentally redresses them in more becoming styles. Has flicker of anxiety over Third-World debt.

Cheryl:
Missing from train. Nothing serious, just a touch of flu, so decided to stay home. Doesn't take chances where her health is concerned although favors nuclear power and sometimes drives through red lights. Go figure.

BUSES

Gordon:
Considers offering woman next to him a stick of sugarless gum, but worries she'll think it's just a stupid conversational gambit. (It is, but she wouldn't mind.) Wishes he could offer her a cigarette—it's sexier and more sophisticated, except for the part about getting a horrible disease and dying in agony—or a sweater set or some fresh baked goods.

Sally:
Imagines that the bus is transported to a deserted island. Decides to mate with the guy three seats up, by the window, if he's a college graduate and has sturdy teeth.

Jane:
Pretends to be listening to her DiscMan to avoid conversation. Has hot date later and is concentrating on maintaining anticipatory sexual arousal. It's working.

. . . .

Carla:
Considers having collagen implants to give herself pouty Euro-lips. Hopes Tom Cruise will play Oliver North in the movie, and that it will be a musical set in a federal prison.

SIDEWALKS

Maurice:
Just got a raise and is walking on air. Doesn't realize his wallet was swiped at the last corner.

Spotty:
Spent a delightful day pawing through trash bins and sniffing things. Hopes the guys at the firehouse won't be angry. (They didn't even notice he was gone.)

SELDOM USED SUBTERRANEAN PASSAGES

Brown (Norway) Rat:
A reverse commuter, he's just now going out to eat and wander around the sewer. Misses the Automat.

THE AIR

Type-A Influenza:
Too small to have a brain, but has an incipient feeling of relief that there's no effective antiviral agent among the current phar-macopoeia.

Ordinary Dust Mote:
Feels inadequate because he's only an inanimate object.

. . . .

SPACELANES

Vzdgkl:
Really enjoyed collecting the soil samples, but is looking forward to getting back to his own planet. Still thinks Dan Quayle's nomination was meant as a joke; doesn't get it.

. . . .

PHOTO FEATURE: THE DUNMORE DECTUPLETS

Attn. art dept.—Here are the captions along with notes on the photos we'd like for "A Visit with the Dunmore Dectuplets," subtitle: "A family album of America's top ten on their third birthday."

PIC: Shirley Dunmore in hospital bed with her ten infants fanned out across her lap, as Jack Dunmore, his arm around his lovely wife, stands there grinning like a boob. Note: touch up as necessary, i.e., no drool!

CAP: "They're quite a handful," smiles Mama on the birth of the nation's first dectuplets. And the proud papa? "It was a shock all right, but they're my kids and I love them all," he asserts in this first published picture of the delectable decs, taken three years ago this month.

PIC: Just two days old, taking a nap. Make sure they don't look like they're dead.

. . . .

CAP: "I want to name half of them for the starting lineup of the 1971 Knicks championship team and the others after the Great Lakes," says Dad, "but Shirl thinks 'Superior' is a stupid name. She wants Mick, Brian, Keith, Bill, and Charley, along with the Five Towns. Baby Hewlett? I ask you!"

PIC: The day they take *les dix* home: the happy parents shake hands with the hospital staff.

CAP: Two-career couple Jack and Shirley Dunmore—he's an attorney, she's an investment analyst—say goodbye to the Fertility Drug Research Team. "We'd put off having a family for a long time," confides the new mother, age 52. "But thanks to these wonderful scientists, we were able to have all the kids we wanted in a single batch, without taking too much time away from the office."

PIC: At six months, decs bare all on bearskin rug. No visible genitalia, please.

CAP: "Jack's mom hopes they'll become doctors—an internist, a cardiologist, ob-gyn, ear nose and throat, a neurologist, a pediatrician, a dermatologist, an opthalmologist, either liver or kidneys, and maybe psychiatry," says Shirley Dunmore. "She'd like them to share a practice. On her block. Of course Jack hopes we'll have another so we can field a football team, but I don't know. It's a little soon to think about more kids, especially now that I'm up for a big promotion."

PIC: Isn't there a shot of them in little mortarboards and tiny black gowns?

CAP: "When they're ready for college, we figure the first year's tuition will run three hundred, three hundred fifty thou-

. . . .

111

sand, around in there," calculates Jack Dunmore. "I think we can handle it if we start saving now, if the kids do well on their Merit Scholarship exams, and if the big one develops a jump shot."

P I C : First birthday. I seem to remember a shot of the ten little publicity hounds in party hats, terrified of ten cupcakes, each with a candle in it.

C A P : "Those are Godiva white chocolate mousse cupcakes, the official dessert of the Dunmore Dectuplets," says a proud and practical Shirley at the decs' first birthday party. "And we're wrapping up negotiations to make Monsieur Paul the official Beaujolais Nouveau," adds a happy Jack. Also in attendance for the festivities, Jason and Melissa Prokosh—he's in laptop computers, she's in cable television—and their own mini-baby-boom, the Prokosh octuplets, previously known as America's Favorite Babies.

P I C : Remember when they did the Marine recruiting poster, around the start of the Central American Action? "We're What You're Fighting For" was the slogan over a photo of them drinking Cokes and "reading" *TV Guide*. Don't we have a shot of them standing in front of it, wearing those Marine hats that are way too big for them?

C A P : From the halls of Montezuma to the teeming streets of Managua, the Dunmore Decs pitched right in when the Caribbean Basin Plan entered a new phase.

P I C : Taking a walk in that stroller-train thing with the billboards on the sides.

. . . .

CAP: A modern containerized port at their nursery school? A massive flood-control program for their backyard? A six-figure fee for consulting on low-income housing? Could be! Out for a stroll with Republican Senate hopefuls, the kids are keeping mum about their endorsement. "But it's quid pro quo, nothing for nothing," jokes dad. "That's the American way—free enterprise! I love this country!"

PIC: The babies at eighteen months, toddling around a mound of ravioli.

CAP: "You should be seeing it on TV in about six weeks," declares a savvy Shirley Dunmore at the press conference announcing the delightful decs' latest commercial tie-in. "You see the kids, and then you see me, and then I say, 'Kids, a career, and Stouffer's ravioli stuffed with lobster meat and covered with cream sauce—a dectuply delicious combination!' Jack and I really do eat it. I'll tell you, if it weren't for Boil-in-Bag Deluxe Dinners, I don't know what we'd do. More take-out, I guess."

PIC: That document-signing at *Commentary*.

CAP: The Dunmore Decs affix their tiny footprints—they're too young to write!—to a petition that the Committee for the Free World will run in the *New York Times* supporting the Central American Action. "We welcome their help," says Midge Decter. "They're real Americans," agrees hubby Norman Podhoretz.

PIC: On the set of their third picture, the kids with their doubles.

CAP: Ten "little people"—they're the ones with the cigars—pose with the decs on location for *Scamps Go South*. Small but

. . . .

113

brave, these highly trained stunt midgets are shown preparing for a dangerous scene in which the bus is strafed as it enters Tegucigalpa.

PIC: Naked babies in pearls and lipstick, heavy mascara, eyeliner—remember, the shot that caused the big stink.

CAP: "We didn't push them into anything," insists a stern Shirley Dunmore. "There's no Brooke Shields story here; nobody is being oiled up for the camera." Adds a solemn father, "This was something they wanted to do, all by themselves. Shirl and I tried not to influence them either way. The kids have always admired Mr. Flynt. They're proud to be associated with any film his company makes. We've read them the script, and they feel those scenes are in good taste and are an integral part of the story."

PIC: Wearing OshKosh B'Gosh overalls, Geraldo joins them in their playpen for a cup of juice.

CAP: "Simple infants or something twisted and evil? Spawn of Satan? Adorable death cult brainwashed by heavy-metal music? Ten of the cuddliest little neo-Nazis ever to spew forth a doctrine of racist filth? Find out on the next 'Geraldo'!"

PIC: Wrap it up with a shot from the third birthday party. If you're not satisfied with what we've got on hand, check with CBS: they had the TV rights, and I'm sure they'll sell us a still.

CAP: Representing a combined thirty baby-years of show business experience, the Dunmore Decs smile professionally at their birthday bash, a gala benefit for the HyperNatality Foundation and the Pro-Family Party. Among their pals helping them

. . . .

celebrate—singer Julio Iglesias, Chrysler prexy Lee Iacocca, dashing Donald Trump, feisty Jeane Kirkpatrick. By fax from the White House comes this message: "Happy birthday to America's babies." We couldn't have put it better!

ALONG
THE FROST BELT

In the older parts of the city, a Façade Advisory is in effect. Public service announcements remind listeners to use caution where concentrations of Beaux-Arts frills and Deco fripperies may maim or even kill with plummeting fragments of frieze, cornice, dentil. Last week, a chunk of masonry just missed Malcolm Holmes's cousin Ernie.

"Damn finial near took his arm off," Malcolm says. "I told him—Ernie, tune to the all-news radio and you'll know where things are falling. But Ernie likes that funk music. Anyhow, we're moving to Phoenix soon, so we'll be able to listen to any damn station we want."

In the loft district, where columns, lintels, arches, even entire façades are mass produced of cast iron, architectural ornaments fall with enough force to crush a bus. Of course, there are no buses; the Transit Department has rerouted them to avoid falling objects. If you are driving home, the T.D. suggests you plan an alternative route along the avenues lined with the glass boxes of the International Style.

. . . .

But for portrait painter Mavis Boulton, this is home: "I loathe that scum Mies van der Rohe and his bleak glass-curtain walls," she declares. "I won't concede to modernism, and I won't relocate in El Paso."

As buildings shift, decay, break apart, nothing in the city remains perpendicular. Geraniums in terra-cotta pots drop from window ledges in unprecedented numbers. Last month eleven deaths were attributed to saplings in wooden tubs tumbling from roof gardens, the first month that tubbed-tree deaths hit double digits. A new municipal ordinance confronts the crisis: within ninety days, all domestic flora must be transplanted to NerfPots or their equivalent. Failure to comply means a fifty-dollar fine.

"We are just poor working people," complains Raffa Naphti, a cab driver. "Where do I find money for these polyfoam pots? I have offered to wrap all of our plants in old newspapers and magazines—we have many back issues of *Vanity Fair, Esquire, USA Today*—but the police say that this is not enough."

Indeed, reading matter itself falls fatally. Book deaths remain high, analysts suggest, because of the continued popularity of *The Herbs of Glen Carron*, a 1,265-page multigenerational family saga. Health officials are encouraging a return to slim volumes of poetry.

"I'll get swift action on the Sara Teasdale subsidy," promises City Councilwoman Ruth Moscowitz.

Caught between rising demands for services and a shrinking economic base, the Council is trying to lure high-tech industry to the area, offering a package of incentives featuring zoning variances, tax abatements, and discount movie coupons. However, the competition for new jobs is fierce, and the Council must vie with metroplexes willing to guarantee prom dates to the children of senior executives.

. . . .

Services are curtailed while the city waits for an economic upturn. In the high schools the student-teacher ratio has ballooned to 275-1, although this year's budget provides megaphones for math and science teachers; that should help get test scores up. Ever since last spring when all the animals were released from city zoos, park usage has declined, trimming maintenance costs, a case of one economy unexpectedly begetting another. However, as more brave souls organize park safaris—some for sport but most to put meat on the table—the feral packs will be thinned, and people will again use the park, to sleep or to forage for nuts and berries. In any case, the cold weather will kill off many of the animals who manage to avoid the hunters, except for the penguins and the polar bears.

Naturally discontent is widespread. "I can't just wait around for the shift to a service economy," sighs Melissa Clifford. "I'm taking a job as an au pair girl in Tokyo. It's room and board and a little pocket money. And who knows—maybe I'll meet a nice guy and, well, there are always possibilities for blondes as tall as I am: five-ten."

For others, discontent takes more radical forms. If local government can't do the job . . . they say, with menacing ellipsis. There are rumors that the United Parcel Service is plotting a coup. The UPS men are a well-organized, highly mobile, uniformed force that could deploy rapidly across the city. Some say they've already armor-plated their familiar brown trucks and installed swivel mounts for .50-caliber machine guns. It is believed that the UPS men have made alliances, arranging for Federal Express to provide air support should the governor order in National Guard troops to retake the city. However, as long as the UPS men don't interrupt the flow of CARE packages from West Germany, the governor is not likely to take any action at all.

· · · · · · · ·

In the meantime, the Buildings Department has issued its latest long-term forecast. Thousands of window-mounted air conditioners, their braces corroding rapidly during the ongoing acidity crisis, will pull loose and crash to the street by year's end. Transit Department spokesmen pledge to complete installation of reinforcing beams in the roofs of all buses and get them back on the street. The City Council will issue each citizen one of the new carbon-fiber safety umbrellas if Mobil will provide another grant.

A Pet Emergency is predicted for tomorrow. Large clumsy dogs—Labs, Belgian sheepdogs, Saint Bernards—are expected to stumble off fire escapes and land on the windshields of passing cars. Cats will dive for pigeons on windowsills, launching themselves from upper floors and causing minor injuries—contusions, abrasions, some broken bones—to pedestrians. City clean-up crews will remain on duty as long as the Pet Watch is in effect. The mayor worries about the overtime payments, but it must be done. Perhaps the union will again accept canned goods in lieu of actual money.

Although the falling seems to be getting worse, life goes on, and people continue to laugh and joke. Today on the all-news radio featurette, "Things That Go Bump," there was the story of a woman whose shoulder was fractured when she was struck by a falling boa constrictor. She found the incident sufficient impetus to return to the bosom of the church whose sacraments she'd forsaken thirty-five years ago. Doctors report that woman and snake are doing fine.

But "Things That Go Bump" is only sixty seconds long, and the rest of the news is not so merry: objects continue to fall. Recently in the theater district, 150 feet of pavement gave way without warning. The huge fissures that continue to lengthen on four major crosstown arteries are now spewing forth plumes

· · · · · · · ·

of unidentified gases. The lava flow in the subway tunnels continues unabated. Several station entrances now belch smoke and ash. The consultants hired to explain the steam pipe eruptions refuse to release their report. And the agronomists flown in by the federal government simply do not know why the grass in the city's parks turns white, withers, and dies.

THE ANNOUNCERS'
CONVENTION

—I've wanted to be an announcer ever since I was a kid. I'd take a banana and pretend it was a microphone. Or a hammer or a shoe, anything longer than it was wide. Lucky I'm no Freudian. Sometimes on Mom's pie day, I'd take her rolling pin and pretend to announce the Jack Benny show. My brother thought I was really stupid. He used to put a colander on his head and pretend to be Kaiser Wilhelm.

—I never wanted to be a DJ or an MC or a sportscaster or a quizmaster or a weather-guy or an anchor or a host: I wanted to be an announcer. You're loafing around the station, but there's that edge, that tension that never dissipates. Suddenly, trouble. You're on. "We are experiencing technical difficulties. Please stand by." It's like baseball, like playing center field. Nearly nothing happens, nearly all of the time, but when it does you'd better be ready or the fans will lob those big paper cups of beer down on your head. The truth is, I even like the routine stuff: Coming up at eleven . . . We'll be right back . . . Stay

. . . .

tuned . . . The preceding was a paid political announcement. It's a great job.

—Announcing school was outstanding! I loved those all-night bull sessions where nothing was out of bounds—could Superman beat Batman in a fair fight; who'd let you touch her breasts; who'd make more, a dentist or a lawyer. During LBJ's tenure some guys said they'd refuse to announce "Ladies and gentlemen, the President of the United States." Unprofessional! You've got a duty to serve; that's not politics, it's patriotism. After all, he was the only President we had. Until, you know, we got Nixon. Those show-offy peaceniks were mostly the Chosen People, which was stupid anyway—like guys that nasal were going to make it as announcers! You've got to sound American; that's a legitimate job requirement.

—Newscasters? The greatest! Yeah, yeah, yeah, I've heard the cracks: What do you call an announcer who owns more than one tweed sport jacket? An announcer with a year-round tan? An announcer with a subscription to both *Time* and *Newsweek*? But those are just jokes: news guys are tops. They're up on current events, and no one can articulate the administration's point of view with more clarity—any administration; that's what being objective is. I'm proud to have a voice even half as mellifluous.

—I'll be telling some story to my wife, and she'll say, "Huh? Speak up! Stop mumbling!" She gets so mad. She says I articulate for total strangers, so why can't I articulate for her? But when I get home I want to kick off my shoes, mispronounce a few place names, and take it easy.

. . . .

—They've got these totally automated mellow-sound radio stations in the Midwest pumping out hour after hour of mall-rock,
and the nearest barrel-chested full-throated man is an hour away
in Salt Lake City—unshaven, bleary-eyed, still in dirty pajamas
at two in the afternoon. Damn right, I'm scared.

Back in school we were pretty cocky. We'd joke that the guys
in the bottom ten percentile would end up with jobs saying,
"Attention K-Mart shoppers . . ." Right now, those seem like
pretty good jobs to me.

—Most of us are still sore about the boycott of the Moscow
Olympics. The games come along once every four years; you
train like a maniac to peak at just the right time. Four years later,
who can say? Maybe you're making your announcements
strapped into a Bell jet pack, reeling with motion sickness, hov-
ering over five hundred Elvis impersonators, and not a Russian
in sight. Even if you make a great one, it'll appear with an
asterisk in the record book. Or four years after that, maybe the
time difference has you introducing the air rifle quarter-finals at
four in the morning while one of Bryant Gumbel's inflatable
suits handles the sexy stuff in prime time—gymnasts, divers,
track and field: you know, the future spokesmen for stockbrok-
ers and breakfast cereal. A lot of announcers are plenty pissed.

—Just before I go on, I'm sure that I'm about to make some
stupid mistake and become famous for it, like that announcer
who introduced "Hoobert Heever." Would you believe it, I can't
recall his name? Any analyst could tell you why. Hoobert
Heever. It's what we call a blooper. Then they put you on a
blooper TV special. Eight p.m. Family hour. Or maybe your slip-
up is a double-entendre. You'll find yourself in some spicy un-

. . . .

censored bloopers movie playing college campuses so some beer-sodden nineteen-year-old can have a few guffaws and a feeling of superiority at your expense.

—It was over at the old Consolidated Network. We'd knock back shots of bourbon and bet a week's pay on tongue twisters. And we'd eat eggs off the belly of a naked audio engineer. I mean if he wasn't naked, you'd get little bits of lint in your food.

—I'm rarely recognized. Now and then a telephone operator spots the voice, but for most calls no operator assistance is required; you can save by dialing direct. There was one time at Howard Johnson's: a waitress called everyone over and had me repeat my order about a dozen times—a clamwich and a HoJo Cola; I still remember. The only thing I can't stand is when somebody says, "You're so much more sibilant in person." I hate that.

—The headline that nobody will ever read is "Hero Announcer Saves Lives at Noisy Mishap." Forget about it. No matter what you do. You risk your larynx and some doctor gets the credit, or a cop, or a fireman. But never the announcer.

—The editors of *Attention Please*, the magazine of radical announcing, would like you to sign this card. It declares that in the event of nuclear war, you'd refuse to announce the evacuation plans. How many signatures? So far, just two. But it's only the third day of the convention.

—What really gets me is people saying George Bush is OK as long as he sticks to the script, as if that were a crime. Let me tell you, pal, I damn well stick to the script, Sir John frigging Gielgud sticks to the script, and for eight years of peace and prosperity, President Ronald M. Reagan stuck to the script! OK, it wasn't an actual script with words to read; it was little drawings, but the principle is the same. And for those eight years that script kept us out of war, except for, you know, the invasion of Trinidad. Grenada? Grenada. And Nicaragua and those marines in Lebanon. And jobs. Thousands of them—more burgers flipped, more fries dunked in boiling fat than ever before in the annals of America!

—It's let me be a witness to history. I remember back in the old days telling folks to turn to Conelrad, 640 and 1240. Of course, it was only a test and not an actual emergency. I've interrupted regularly scheduled programming in the glad times—like the walk on the moon—and the sad times—like the Mayaguez incident, the Pueblo affair, the U-2 spy plane incident, the Iran-contra affair, the downing of the Iranian airliner, which I happen to think was totally and completely different than when the Russians shot down KAL 007. I could give you a hundred reasons. I've got them right here on this wallet card the FCC sent us.

—For breakfast? I had white toast with margarine, a bowl of oatmeal, a glass of skim milk. I drove to work in a beige sedan, a four-door. I'm about average height, medium build, brown hair, brown eyes. I wear a brown suit. I get to the job and I read things that others have written for me. I'm not the actual program, you see, I'm just a peripheral. I don't even use my own voice; I use my announcing voice so I sound like I don't come from anyplace at all. That's what you want me to say, isn't it?

. . . .

HIS RUN
FOR THE ROSES

It's when Jason finishes his daily workout that Connie takes over; she's a hot-walker at a four-furlong track near Smithtown, Long Island. "By the end of the run he's pretty lathered up," she says. "I lead him around while he cools off, then I wash him down with a bucket and squeegee. I toss a blanket over him and strap on the feedbag. Usually I fill it with chocolate pudding; he really goes for that."

He's earned it. Jason Blaylock is training hard to be the first boy to win the Kentucky Derby.

"The rules specify a three-year-old: Jason is a three-year-old," says his father, Harold Blaylock. "They don't say anything about horses. If the Racing Commission bars the boy, we fight. But this isn't about settling out of court for the big money, or licensing Jason's picture for toys or T-shirts. The point isn't a made-for-TV movie called *The Kid with the Thoroughbred Heart*. It's about making the American child competitive again."

Competitive, perhaps. But victorious? Mike Callahan, turf reporter for *Newsday*, the Blaylocks' local paper, has seen Jason

. . . .

126

run. He figures it this way: "Twenty-five to one, the kid doesn't finish. A hundred to one against his finishing ahead of any horse. I make it even money that he cries, and eight to five that some child welfare agency intervenes before post time."

Jason's mother, Diane Blaylock, disagrees. "I've seen parents enter a child in a claiming race. This I would never do. To me it is virtually baby selling. That's where the state should intercede. But as long as my son wants to race, I say, 'Run, Jason, Run'—like the cereal jingle which, by the way, he really does eat."

All of this can be tough on what you must remind yourself is just a little boy.

"This one time we went to Saratoga for practice," Jason recalls, "and I lost. I hated that. I hadn't lost before. Of course I'd mostly raced kids my own age, never horses. And this big one, Deconstructionist, kicked a lump of dirt right into my belly. On purpose. It really hurt."

"Sure it hurt," his father, Harold, agrees, "but the boy's got guts, just like me. When I was Jason's age my pop took me down to Nogales every weekend and matched me against the best fighting cocks in the state of Sonora. All the kids in the neighborhood were jealous of that red Schwinn bicycle I bought with my winnings, and of my really neat bandages."

This yeasty spirit has been part of the American character since the early days of the republic, Harold asserts. "Aaron Burr is known to have killed three children, each under age nine, in duels. There was perhaps a fourth, although his death may have been the inadvertent outcome of a bear–boy wrestling match, a popular eighteenth-century recreation."

Concerned parents like the Blaylocks find eager allies in Washington, where the Competitive American Child could become

. . . .

the buzzword of the nineties if some neologism could reduce to a single term what is still very much a phrase. "For too many of our kids," laments one rustbelt Republican, "It's just play, play, play. Of course, it's easy to be a Jeremiah, but I've got new solutions, more like a Joshua. First, industry must do its part. Repealing antiquated child-labor laws won't mean much unless, when kids get back to the factory, they find machines that fit their little hands. That means smaller paint sprayers, arc welders, stamping machines. Then, don't lower the driving age; eliminate it. Tall enough to reach the pedals, tall enough to hit the Interstate. Let's get government off the back of our kids."

Jason Blaylock is not waiting for Congress to act, and neither is his sister, Heather, a cheerful five-year-old who works hard and still finds time to play store, although she calls it "Gallery. This is a Schnabel. It costs a million-zillion dollars. I keep seventy-five percent."

In two households devoted to accomplishment, Heather is thriving. "When I stay at my dad's place in the city," she says, "I have this really small room, but it's got oxygen-enriched air and sleep-teaching tapes. Sometimes I substitute a Debbie Gibson tape, so now I know all her songs by heart, but mostly it's art history. Daddy believes in total immersion. I have a 'precocious grasp of the investment potential of the neo-expressionists'; that's what Ms. Califano wrote on my student evaluation."

A teacher's encouragement is a powerful motivation for the striving child, so acceptance at a top pre-school is important to parents like the Wootens of Bethesda, Maryland. "They don't go just by test scores," says Lois Wooten. "They want a well-rounded child. I'd say that Tim Junior's boxing shows initiative few four-year-olds possess. You know, Mike Tyson's been ducking him for over a year. We're not stupid. We know Little Tim risks concussion, a detached retina, some pretty gruesome internal injuries. But the little guy wants to try, and we think he deserves that chance."

He does indeed, agrees Gary Furman, a pre-school admissions officer disturbed by the many kids who offer him a bribe to avoid the physical exam, or at least the endurance test on the whirling centrifuge. "If a kid can't take a couple of G's, if he's scared to learn exactly where he blacks out, then this school isn't for him.

"And incidentally they're such childish bribes—thirty-two cents, a GI Joe doll with a missing arm, half a Snickers. Don't their parents teach them anything? They'll be in high school before they learn to slip a discreetly folded twenty to a maitre d' or arrange a commission for a foreign official. We've got a long way to go."

And the way to get there, Furman believes, is for parents to become partners in their children's education. "Today's four-year-old is very sophisticated. He or she thinks, 'So what if I earn only a B plus? I'll still get dinner.' But when your child knows that a subpar performance means, not slow starvation, of course, but a drastic reduction in vitamin C—then you'll see improvement. A brush with scurvy is a powerful teaching tool."

None of this surprises the Blaylocks, who decided a long time ago that their kids would be achievers. "Oh my, yes," agrees Harold. "Back when we were still married. To each other, I mean. We'd just started the kids in babyrobics over at the micromall."

"It's funny," Diane interrupts, "because it's really the worst mall out here. I mean the minimalls at least have Mary Boone Artiques, but this place had nothing. Except an excellent toddler workout."

"That's when we began preparing Jason for the Derby," adds Harold, "and even after our separation, we stuck with it."

"I wish we could show you some videotape of the early train-

. . . .

ing," says Diane, "but the machine hasn't been fixed since Jason tried to play back a peanut butter sandwich."

"We've got tape of his first appearance promoting the Full Gallop running shoe," Harold says. "It was terrific. The band played 'My Old Kentucky Home,' and then segued into 'I'm a Little Teapot,' Jason's unofficial theme song. Although, since his trainer had him on the steroids, he'd gotten pretty husky, so the 'short and stout' line kind of embarrassed him."

"It was just so cute!"

"And he was still a little banged up from when this horse, Appropriated Image, had crushed a very small bone in Jason's foot during a practice run down at Hialeah."

"He lost there, too. But overcoming failure is the true test of a baby's character, on and off the field."

"That's what it's all about," says Harold. "Raising a child you can be proud of. So maybe he doesn't capture the Triple Crown. I can live with that. No baby, no matter how multi-talented, has come even this close—not Liza Minnelli, not Robert Longo, not even Sting. Just so Jason does his best."

And after Churchill Downs?

"There ought to be a way for the over-threes to enjoy inter-species competition," says Harold Blaylock. "That's how Jason got the idea for the Michelob Dog–Boy Triathlon. (He doesn't actually have a contract with a brewery; I'm speaking hypothetically. Oh, and girls too.)

"First, the running. Granted: the dog has an edge. The swimming could go either way. Then the cycling, and it's bye-bye, Fido. An exciting comeback for the boy! Of course, if it's too one-sided, we'll alter the bikes to give the dogs a chance. Maybe a big hamster-wheel kind of thing. Whatever makes it fun for Jason. Because, after all, that's who this is for."

. . . .

DAVE LOBEL'S LOVE HOTEL

THE INTRAMARITAL AFFAIR

At the Dog and Baby, a Brooklyn Heights bar, Claudia confides in Yuri. "I want to get that sexual electricity back into bed with Andy."

Yuri pictures Claudia in black silk, rubbing balloons against her hair to build up a static charge. "You wrote that on the questionnaire?" he asks.

"Just gave it a number. 'Arrange in order of importance to your happiness.' I made 'revitalize marital relations' number one. 'Read more' got a seven. I gave a nine to something about having nicer sweaters."

Yuri doubts that a survey was distributed at the university data center where Claudia works. Who'd answer truthfully? Who'd know what the truth was? "If I knew how to increase my supply of happiness, I'd never have bought a twenty-six-inch TV," he says. "I'd have got the nineteen but with remote control." Yuri believes that Claudia's confession of marital discontent signals her desire to resume their affair after a nine-year hiatus. Her husband, Andy, suspects that she already has.

Dave Lobel has seen the questionnaires. They convinced him that millions of midmarriage couples are eager to hypereroticize their lives without endangering their unions. But apartments are small, child care expensive, the Caribbean distant. There's no easy escape. That's how he conceived the Four-Hour Vacation. It begins the moment you check into Dave Lobel's Love Hotel.

HER PLACE

Six months ago, Claudia began an affair with Edward, a news writer for the local ABC station. Andy, a painter, often lectures at colleges around the country, but this wasn't one of those times. While Claudia and Edward stretched out on her couch, thrilled and guilty, Andy was at his studio having a light-bondage liaison with Tomiko Yamashita, his gallery's accountant. Claudia doesn't know that Andy sometimes only pretends to travel, although she assumes he sleeps with students when he's out of town. As long as she needn't acknowledge his infidelities or imply that he has her permission, she was prepared to preserve the illusion of deception. But lately she dislikes their arrangement. It wasn't fair to be denied erotic intensity just because she doesn't travel on business, as if sex were a frequent-flier bonus. And why should she do all the work of Andy's deceit? She doesn't even iron his shirts. Then she met Edward.

"I felt terribly guilty having him at our apartment," she eventually told Yuri, "a feeling I adored. But even something that exciting isn't worth the risk of discovery. Betrayal at home requires unrelenting neatness: no unusually full ashtray, no disheveled sheets. I want to be a little out of control, not passionately tidy."

. . . .

HIS PLACE

Sex at Edward's apartment gave Claudia archeological insights about his girlfriend, Nina—this selfish shampoo, these irresponsible shoes, that lazy jar of pennies. Claudia didn't want Nina to take on greater clarity, preferring her vague, like a deputy mayor at the center of a city scandal Claudia wasn't really following, just glancing at in the headlines.

Trysts at Edward's stirred her sadistic urges; Claudia didn't like that. One afternoon she tossed a crumpled pair of her panties under the bed for Edward—or Nina—to stumble across. Another time she rubbed just a little lipstick in a non-Nina color on the hem of a pillowcase. Edward began to seem so bullyable.

THE INTERMARITAL AFFAIR

In a taxi heading uptown, Dave Lobel dictates into a microcassette. "Assume tristate success and begin planning Love Hotel franchise. Like good pizza and bad croissants, family fun zones will become ubiquitous. Theme parks have peaked; waterparks are dead; fireparks haven't caught on. (Radio ad: "From the moment you don the asbestos safety suit, you'll live the excitement of Wild Fire, America's favorite family flame park.") People are ready for something adult with plenty of parking, a play area for the kids, a leather'n'lace boutique. Put the "mmm" back in marriage.

A FRIEND'S PLACE

"If I wanted to have sex in Eric Keller's apartment," said Claudia, "I'd have an affair with Eric Keller."

. . . .

133

On the other end of the phone Edward made noises of disappointment to disguise his surprise. He'd assumed that she'd already slept with Keller. He was relieved by her demurrer because now he wouldn't have to confide in Eric. Evading opportunities for self-revelation was the basis of their enduring friendship.

Still, he was charmed by her distaste for his friend, savoring its contrast with her warmer feelings for himself. Claudia, detecting his pleasure, suspected that what Edward relished is the suspicion that she holds him in similar contempt. At any rate, Eric's bed is much too small.

AN ODD INFIDELITY

"Before Edward, I never had affairs," Claudia tells Yuri at Men-in-Furs, a pro-athlete hangout on the East Side. "When my sexual yearnings became overpowering, I'd let a man buy me clothes. Never expensive and never crudely intimate—no teddies or tap pants. But he had to pick it out, watch me try it on, and pay for it. Weeks later, when I'd wear that belt or tank top, I'd get dizzy from the heat."

LOVE NOTES

Dave believes that, as at Jack La Lanne's, lunch hour will be busy. Two-career couples meet for a midday romp while the kids are in school—not just an intensely erotic marriage-buttressing experience, but also a missed meal, saving many calories for later deployment on elaborate desserts.

He distributes customer preference cards at a popular infidelity hotel near campus. They ask: What excuse do you give your spouse for your absence? The most common response: I'm teaching a course at the New School. It's perfect for a weekly liaison. Unlikely midnight phone calls are from "a student." The school's famous meager wages explain the paucity of moonlighting money.

WORKPLACE

Years of monogamy have refined Edward and Claudia's sexual response to thrive in the particular environment of their marriages. Alter that erotic niche and they become confounded. They had bad sex in various settings, awkward and bemused like kangaroos in the snow.

Edward shares an office with Carlos, who lingers interminably each evening. With Carlos in the room, Edward can barely face making a personal phone call. His excessive modesty thwarts the erotic possibilities of his Formica-topped desk, his hideous swivel chair, his execu-shag carpet. He suffers interoffice impotence; it's undoubtedly temporary.

Claudia's office has an open plan. She imagines dozens of legs extended over the four-foot partitions, a loopy, job-related lovers' lane. Security guards come around with nosy flashlights, tap on the panels, and order everyone back to work. She becomes occupationally unresponsive and rereads the workers' compensation law.

They meet at a midtown hotel catering to business travelers and feel guilty, less for deceiving their spouses than for implying they're on the job: they'd betrayed their bosses.

They consider a hot-bed motel out by the airport. Claudia is uneasy about an evening that begins in Manhattan and proceeds to Queens: isn't that backwards? They rent a car and drive for

. . . .

an hour to encounter a snickering clerk and an all-wrong in-room pornographic movie that makes them want to forswear sex forever. There's a waterbed in the room; Edward notices algae growing inside it. The ride home takes two hours; Claudia gets carsick.

THE MARITAL BED

Cat out, answering machine on, diaphragm in, newspapers all over the floor. Claudia and Andy feel tender and generous. He's a sweet guy, she thinks. This is a nice way to live, he thinks.

"It's the aphrodisiac ink of the Sunday *Times*," says Claudia.

"I was imagining your thighs all through the Week in Review," Andy replies.

"Or maybe something in the maple syrup," she says.

"No. I had eggs."

"So it's the ink?"

"Definitely." says Andy. "They use a different ink for the daily edition."

"They have to or nobody would go to work."

"Maybe I'll watch a little of the game."

"How quick do you think I can do the acrostic?"

"It'll take you more than thirty-five minutes."

"For a quarter?"

"It's a bet."

Fledgling, the cat, scratches at the door, wanting to be let back into the bedroom. The phone rings.

"Oh damn," she says, "I'll bet it's a relative."

"The machine's still on," he says.

"Great."

. . . .

DAVE'S WONDERFUL WEEK

Monday his *Newsweek* cover appears, "The Hip Howard Johnson." Tuesday night downtown, frosty blondes invite him to
the ladies' room for drugs and kisses, but he just says no.
Wednesday he learns that his book, *Hot Husbands, Wild Wives*,
will hit number one on Sunday's *Times* best-seller list. He's con-
gratulated the next day at a White House lunch, a stately display
of bonhomie and malapropisms. Celebrated for domesticating a
nation's anarchic libido, he reaps a post-cholesterol bonanza
from the American Dairy Council when, on Friday, he endorses
Love Butter: "You needn't eat it to enjoy!" He begins the weekend by watching "Wifelings," the popular cartoon show he's
producing. He spends Sunday in bed with a supermodel; her
husband's got National Guard duty.

AN IMPETUOUS CONFESSION

Claudia and Yuri meet for drinks at The Bull's Behind, a bar
associated with unspeakable interspecies perversions.

"I've been married for nine years," she begins, "so why do
so many men—"

"Listen, Claudia," Yuri interrupts. "Before you go any further,
there's something you should know about Edward and Andy
and me."

BREZHNEV GONE, FORGOTTEN

FOR RUSSIANS, BREZHNEV IS A FADING MEMORY

—headline, *New York Times*

"The big Zil limo, the apartment on Kutozovsky Prospekt, the dacha in Uspenskoye—that was him, wasn't it?" reminisced a Novosibirsk bus driver.

"Who could forget? It was in 1978—no, 1979—the time I saw him in person. He was giving a speech, I think, or performing a folk dance of an autonomous republic," commented a retired miner in Bratsk.

"He had that nice dog," recalled a soldier on station in Petropavlovsk, "or was that Khrushchev?"

For many Russians, these scattered recollections are all that remain of their former leader, and official commemorations do not go much further. Named after Mr. Brezhnev are a clarinet factory in Murmansk; a driving school in Chelyabinsk; a proposed town north of the Arctic Circle; a rental rowboat, one of a fleet of thirty-five available to anyone for a few rubles an hour

· · · · · · · ·

on the artificial lake in Moscow's Gorky Park; and a sandwich, smoked sturgeon on black bread, in one of the capital's not particularly popular delicatessens.

"Since he died? Maybe three or four fellows have ordered a Leonid," sighs the counterman. "One of them sent it back."

In the hours immediately following his death, there was hope that things might be different for the architect of détente. A rumor flashed through the country: the Politburo would seek production of an American-made miniseries. Bruce Boxleitner's name was mentioned by *Izvestia*; the cultural attaché in Washington was consulted about William Devane. Yet somehow the film was never made. A decent step-deal was signed; the Presidium approved both the outline and the treatment, but no shooting script exists. Or if it does, it's lost somewhere in the murky corridors of the Kremlin. Experts at the U.S. State Department recognized that Leonid Brezhnev had been consigned to oblivion the day that Valerie Bertinelli received her unconditional release and accepted a role as mob wife in an American prime-time soap opera.

There were other signs. The brevity of the official period of mourning—from 11:30 a.m. on the day of the funeral until 12:25 that same afternoon—underscored how quickly glory can fade in a system that still cherishes only one of its former leaders, Lenin. This becomes apparent when you enter a state-run gift shop for a souvenir of the capital—if you have foreign currency, of course. Such shops are not for the ordinary Russian, who must seek his novelty ashtray, his comical T-shirt, his ribald coffee mug on the black market. Nor will you find, as you search the stalls offering *strovskaya*, unauthorized celebrity biographies, a tell-all quickie penned by his driver or mistress, his barber or bodyguard.

While the great man lay in state, the Soviet Bureau of Labor

. . . .

Statistics spotted anomalies in their figures, suggesting that the entire nation had thrown itself into its work in an effort to forget.

"It's the best way to deal with grief," shrugs an apparatchik, "to cope with the anguish of separation. There's mercy in it, and many extra metric tons of specialty steels."

To a citizen of the United States, where late-Kennedy-related industries employ many thousands of people and contribute a hefty percentage to the GNP, the Soviet Union can seem a heartless place divorced from its own past. Americans must remember that, despite its military might, the Soviet Union is still in many respects a developing nation with little time to squander on nostalgia. "Don't look back," runs a popular saying in the Ukraine, "you might trip over a cabbage." And so there was no special issue of *People* magazine for Leonid Brezhnev. Ironically, there is no *People* at all in this people's republic.

In America experts try to assess this Great National Forgetting. What does it presage for Yuri Andropov's place in Soviet history, now that he has assumed the role of a formerly living person, albeit one who only recently wielded vast political power? And how will it affect the policies of Konstantin Chernenko, once an aging member of the old guard and now, at least officially, in a postactive state? For Andropov and Chernenko, it may be too late. Under the Soviet system, there is little the deceased can do. For Mikhail Gorbachev, however, several options are available.

"He is in a curiously contradictory position," asserts one psychokremlinologist. "In some ways he is relieved to see Brezhnev forgotten. You don't want to hear your wife reminisce about the sexual prowess of her first husband, do you? This is how Mikhail feels. No one wishes to compete with the dead; you can't win. The dead never drink too much at parties, insult their hostess, trample salted nuts into the carpet. The living are more fallible, as I tried to explain to my wife just last night."

. . . .

So Gorbachev is glad to see Brezhnev forgotten?

"I'm reluctant to speculate without seeing him in a clinical setting; it's risky to make a diagnosis based only on high-resolution satellite photographs. However, Gorbachev recognizes himself as a potentially dead person and, as such, he longs to see Brezhnev remembered. He yearns for an upsurge in monument construction, an epidemic of nostalgia, scattered outbreaks of ancestor worship. He pines for his nation to live in the past, just as soon as he becomes a part of that past. But at the same time, he doesn't want anyone getting sentimental over his predecessors.

"These are perfectly natural feelings; I'm sure he'll learn to externalize them in socially acceptable ways. I'd look for deeper cuts in Warsaw Pact armored divisions, but would anticipate continued turmoil in Latvia. Although I project only modest improvements in the Russian grain harvest—1 to 3 percent this year—I believe that Gorbachev's doctrine of perestroika is fundamentally sound. But this is only guesswork. I don't even know what medication he's on. Pharmacokremlinology is way out of my field."

Last spring, the word "chubby" appeared in a *Pravda* editorial, the first official criticism of Brezhnev. A small article buried on page 27 of *Izvestia* suggested that he talked about himself all the time and never asked anybody how things were going with them. Only hours after his son-in-law was sentenced for corruption, demolition began on the Brezhnev Clarinet Works in Murmansk. Radio signals intercepted by the National Security Agency suggest the imminent construction on that site of the Gerald Ford Bottling Works; it may produce millions of liters of Miller Lite.

. . . .

AFTER
THE AFFAIR

Ironically, it may actually have brought us closer together, clearing the air and getting things out into the open. These days we speak to each other with candor and compassion and yet, paradoxically, my crime has tainted every interaction with distrust, psychic pain, and barely veiled hostility. I must accept that it may be years before she can ask me the time without verifying my reply on her own watch.

Experts say this incident will make us realize that our life together is the most important thing we have. When I consider how close I came to destroying it, not only with my extramarital liaisons, but also by taking her for granted, well, I get chills. The cheating and exposure, the confrontation and remorse have provided the stimulus I needed to awaken me from my domestic somnambulism. Not that my marriage is the only important thing in my life—I've got a good job, nice friends; I play squash; I enjoy keeping up with current events; and I like to read, mostly biographies. But yes, marriage is number one. On a long and varied list. Also, I listen to music on compact discs.

. . . .

What most surprised me, after the screaming, the accusations, the bitterness, was how sexually appealing I began to find my wife. The air crackled and hummed with an erotic charge I hadn't felt since our courtship days. Almost as startling was the way these periods of intense desire alternated with weeks, months even, when she held no charm whatever. It was a peculiar kind of indifference, like seeing your favorite program listed in *TV Guide*, but it's a rerun.

Somehow we go on. A month later we were buying a big queen-sized bed. We also picked up a card table and four chairs. We'd been meaning to for years, and finally we said why wait for a sale? Let's just do it.

You undergo a kind of wrenching, an emotional upheaval, a cleansing fire: after that nothing can ever be the same. This morning on the radio, I heard the mayor say, "I know exactly how I'm doin'—lousy! Most of my closest associates are in disgrace if not actually in jail. The city's bridges are coming down around my ears. The schools are a dangerous travesty, and the streets are filled with pathetic beggars. What am I, wacko? I know I blew it!"

Is anything more labyrinthine than the human heart? Lost in its myriad chambers, anyone might need help; that's no disgrace. I'm ready to consult an expert, a factory-trained mechanic with the specialized tools and computer-controlled diagnostic equipment that will have my car running showroom perfect.

Less talk, more rock—it's a goal, something to strive for. A man needs a sense of direction if he is to move forward. Sure, he has to admit his mistakes, but he also must allow himself to feel good again, to enjoy a sense of progress, to say yes, I bought a wonderful CD player with chest-pounding bass and sizzling treble. You see, every sunset is a sunrise—you know, for the

· · · · · · · ·

people who live to your west. Where you are now, it's definitely getting darker.

There is not a precise moment when it begins; it creeps up on you gradually until one afternoon as the sun settles onto the horizon, the wind picks up, there's a chill in the air; suddenly you realize that your fur has thickened and turned white to provide warmth and camouflage on the snowy ridges of a harsh Arctic landscape where winter is as fierce and unforgiving as the new brand of Islamic fundamentalism spreading across the Third World, only dimly understood in the West where analysts await the decline of the Imams and the revival of the accordion, popping up with toe-tapping infectiousness in New Orleans zydeco music, new-wave polkas, and in the Tex-Mex bands that have been unable to dislodge Panamanian strongman Manuel Noriega. Despite an arms embargo, a devastated economy, and the creation of no-calorie fats like Olestra, he remains a twelve-year-old boy who suddenly finds himself in the body of an adult, undetectable by enemy radar because of the application of stealth technology and comfortable soft contact lenses that give even brown-eyed patients the blue, the violet, or the greenhouse effect, producing a global warming trend linked to atmospheric pollutants and the build-up of carbon dioxide, causing skin to redden, blister, and crack—a cheap, potent, smokable form of cocaine laying waste our cities and bringing us tantalizingly near the long-sought goal of a room-temperature superconductor, the key to magnetically levitating trains speeding along silently, unlimited inexpensive electric power, and an ever widening H.U.D. scandal miring dozens of former Reagan officials in charges of pervasive corruption and stimulating a spiral of violence in our baseball parks. You do what you can—curtail beer sales, put on extra security personnel—to thwart the emergence

. . . .

144

of British-style soccer hooliganism that could result in the lowest possible rating from *Consumer Reports*, alleging a tendency to tip over during sharp turns even at low speed, charges that are vigorously denied by a spokesman for Drexel Burnham Lambert, whose research efforts have yielded startling photographs of nineteen-year-old Norma Jean Baker—Marilyn Monroe—then a lovely, fresh-faced brunette threatening to disrupt the Seoul Olympics with acts of terrorist violence likely to generate still longer delays at America's airports, intensifying an already catastrophic nursing shortage coupled with a debt crisis too complex to be neatly summarized on Chris Whittle's Channel One —twelve minutes of bland headlines, candy bar commercials, and large public atriums offered to junior high schools in exchange for a package of tax abatements and a favorable ruling from a Supreme Court bent on dismantling a hundred years of civil rights legislation and ordering a shift to cars that run on methanol, easing America's dependence on the thuggish innuendos of Lee Atwater and presenting a constant threat to shipping in the Persian Gulf.

What marriage could endure this onslaught of temptation? Is it any wonder I strayed?

A NOTE ABOUT THE AUTHOR

Randy Cohen was born in Charleston, South Carolina, and
grew up in Reading, Pennsylvania. The winner of three Emmy
awards for his writing on "Late Night with David Letterman,"
he lives in New York City with his wife, Katha Pollitt,
and their daughter, Sophie.

A NOTE ON THE TYPE

The text of this book was set in Palatino, a type face designed
by the noted German typographer Hermann Zapf. Named
after Giovanbattista Palatino, a writing master of Renaissance
Italy, Palatino was the first of Zapf's type faces to be
introduced in America. The first designs for the face were
made in 1948, and the fonts for the complete face were issued
between 1950 and 1952. Like all Zapf-designed type faces,
Palatino is beautifully balanced and exceedingly readable.

Composed by Crane Typesetting Service, Inc.,
Barnstable, Massachusetts.

Printed and bound by R. R. Donnelley & Sons,
Harrisonburg, Virginia.

Designed by Valarie Jean Astor.